Self confidence training

>>>————————<<<

A practical guide on how to face your fears and build unshakable self-esteem. Step outside your comfort zone, reach your goals and finally master your life! For men and women

>>>————————<<<

written by Sebastian O'Brien

To whom is trying to find a way to take the driver seat of their life:

Good luck.

table of contents

Introduction — 01

Chapter 1 — 07
No one can make you feel inferior without your consent

Chapter 2 — 26
Setting goals is your road to the life you want

Chapter 3 — 51
You can, you should, and if you're brave enough to start, you will

Chapter 4 — 74
Facing your fears gives you strength, courage and confidence

Chapter 5 — 94
Take action and get to know yourself better

Chapter 6 — 119
You've got to experience failure to understand that you can survive it

Chapter 7 — 144
Believe you can and you're already halfway there

Conclusions — 165

Introduction

Congratulations! The fact that you picked up this book shows that you are already well aware that self-confidence is crucial in almost every aspect of life. It completely transforms both how we see ourselves, and how we are perceived by others - which means everything when it comes to our successes in life; whether in a professional or a personal context. To appear competent or worth someone's time, we must first believe our own hype. After all, if we are not even sure of ourselves, how on earth can we hope to convince others of our value?

You may feel shy, anxious, or simply fearful to change your current daily reality. You want to make something of yourself, but worry that you will fall flat on your face. You may ask yourself if it is really worth it to even try.

If you are unsuccessful this time, won't you be ashamed forever? Will other people remember you for it?

The answer to these questions, quite simply, is *no.* You cannot and should not go through life dwelling on every setback. If you fail, it means you took a risk and tried something. And whatever the outcome, this is something to be proud of, and to never stop doing.

And no, harsh as it may sound, nobody will remember every detail of what you did in your life - what went well and what didn't. As humans, we have a tendency to simplify things and look for the bigger picture. We cannot remember every detail about someone anyway, so we instinctively develop summaries about the people we know. And these summaries are what come to mind whenever we think about them.

So don't waste your energy worrying about the small stuff! You should aim to present the best version of yourself, sure, but fretting over every minor setback, or what you view as your weaknesses, will not help you to do this. Obsessing over your insecurities only draws attention to them but true self-confidence will outshine them. So if you focus on your strengths and find ways to thrive despite - or even because of - these "flaws," then the bigger picture others see will be an impressive one indeed.

Besides, we all spend *far* too much time and energy fretting over what others think about our every move. In truth, we are all more concerned about our own journey. Are you really lying awake at night thinking about how your acquaintance, Sally, tried to set up that catering business last year and it failed? Of course not - you're too focused on your own ambitions and challenges. And so, dear reader, is Sally.

If we all came to terms with the fact that most people really aren't thinking all that much about us - at least not in the way that we fear - then we would all feel a whole lot braver to think big and aim high.

Let me briefly introduce myself before we go any further. My name is Sebastian O'Brien and I was born in Ireland, 1969. I am a Psychotherapist and counselor with many years of experience working to support a whole range of individuals who are ready to finally live life in the driver's seat. I like to work in partnership with my clients to create an environment of good energy and trust. Working with individuals struggling with their self-confidence, to make a real difference in their lives, is what I truly love to do. And this is why I have written the self-confidence training you see before you.

The purpose of this book is to encourage you to believe in yourself. To not give up on your aspirations. To have the success you crave and deserve, and ultimately - to be happy. I will give you all the tools, perspective, and motivation you need to unlock the potential that's already within you, bursting to get out. And all of this is contained within one small but mighty term: *self-confidence.*

There's a common saying that it's not what we do that we will regret most, but what we *don't* do. Do you really want to live with regrets that you didn't follow your dreams, simply due to fear of how other people - who are mostly as anxious and uncertain as you are, believe me - would react if you failed once or twice?

You already have the raw materials to make your life truly marvellous - you just have to make the choice to use them. Alternatively, you can simply live passively, and just "get by," letting life happen to you without taking any real control over it. But life is beautiful. It is the greatest present you have ever and will ever receive. This is why you must take action: grab the pen and write your life as you have always dreamed it to be.

If you haven't reached your goals yet, you may simply need this little push in the right direction to get the ball rolling. You need to focus on yourself; to start a journey of self-discovery for a deeper understanding of what you can improve and change about how you view yourself, how you interact with others - and all the day-to-day challenges that you will face throughout your life.

We are all wonderfully different individuals - but in the way that counts, we all are the same. And so, we all react the same way to the right input. This book will provide you with that input. I will help you to find balance between self-confidence and humility. Between striving for the best and accepting your setbacks. Between pushing your limits and being forgiving and kind to yourself.

I believe that by developing awareness and moving beyond temporary "quick fixes" and instead implementing long-lasting changes - you can better develop the skills and attitudes that will help you lead a more gratifying life.

Let me give you an example I like to use with many clients who struggle with self-belief. Do you know who Edison was - yes, Thomas Edison? Well, when he was still in school, his teacher said that he was "too stupid" to be able to learn anything. As you may have heard, in 1878, he went on to invent the long-lasting commercially viable incandescent lightbulb. Edison's original "lightbulb moment" had a *huge* impact on society. He quite literally lit up the world, and held 1,093 patents to his name by the time of his death. But do you think it was easy for him? Not at all. He failed thousands of times trying to make his dream a reality. But for both his and for all our sakes - thank goodness he didn't give up so easily.

I could offer you hundreds of examples like this one - but that's beside the point. The point is that y*ou* are the only one who can control your own life. You can reach anything - despite what others may have led you to believe during your life. Of course, in this world nothing is plain sailing, but with great dedication and hard work, you can do it - whatever "it" may be for you.

I am not, I regret to inform you, selling a ticket to paradise or offering you everything you desire on a plate. However, if you overcome the self-doubt you're currently grappling with - and you put in all the necessary effort, you will be able to reach it for yourself. This is my promise.

Ultimately, I will show you how to tap into a new realm of self-confidence to transform your passive life into an active one.

To help you in this you will find self-analysis exercises at the end of each chapter. They may seem easy at first glance, but they are really important to get the most out of this book as possible. They are not the types of exercises where you walk away with a grade or score- but simply with a better understanding of the workings of your own mind. Before improving your self-confidence, you must get to deeply know yourself.. If you take them seriously, they are a powerful tool for self-analysis and becoming a better person.

Live every single moment at your full capacity, and you won't have any regrets. Self-confidence is the key to success.

Chapter 1

No one can make you feel inferior without your consent

Let's get started with some definitions. Self-confidence, self-esteem, self-efficacy, and self-acceptance... aren't they all essentially the same thing?

You will, no doubt, have an overall picture of what we're talking about when we mention these terms. But I find that a basic understanding of the subtle differences - the specific areas of self-worth which they cover - is a great way to recognize which areas you struggle with personally. Most likely, you are stronger in some areas than others, but are not sure which. This can make it unclear how to pinpoint your areas for improvement.

Well, let's break it down:

Self-Confidence

You may feel like this one is a no-brainer, but researchers actually have a tough time recognizing on what, exactly, self-confidence is. Some say it's merely "believing in yourself," while others go into more detail about the expectations you have for your life and capabilities, and your subconscious self-evaluation. For non-academic purposes, however, to be self-confident is essentially to trust in our own abilities and believe that we can do whatever we set our minds to.

Along with shaping the beliefs you hold about yourself, self-confidence is a trait that permeates your thoughts, feelings, and actions. Think about a confident person you know. Okay - now have a think about *how* you know this person is confident. You can't know for sure what someone is thinking or feeling, so you base your judgment of their self-confidence on their words, actions, or overall demeanor. You should have at least some degree of self-belief to have self-confidence, but of course - this isn't the whole story.

Why Self-Confidence is so Important

The more confident you become, the more you will be able to quieten the voice inside you that says, "*I can't,*" replacing it with louder and more positive affirmations, being able to reassure yourself of your worth and capacities, completely independently of any external praise or validation. In other words, compliments from others are great, and all, but our self-worth can't depend on this kind of feedback. We must discover for ourselves how to be completely self-reliant when it comes to self-confidence in order to strengthen it. Otherwise, although you may feel unstoppable after some positive feedback, on the reverse side of the coin, the slightest negative reaction can completely floor you.

As social creatures, we tend to feel good when approved and validated by those around us. And although this is not essentially unhealthy, ranking our entire value according to the opinions of others is a surefire way to never feel truly satisfied or self-confident. We will constantly seek praise as an external confirmation that we are good enough. This is a trap we all fall into, at least occasionally. But why do we value the opinions of others so much more than our own in this way? Why isn't our own approval enough?

Because we lack self-confidence!

And of course - the social media revolution has only intensified this obsession with how we're perceived, as we base our self-worth upon the superficial representations of ourselves online. This may be your Facebook profile picture, your satirical tweet, or your LinkedIn bio - the craving for approval is the common thread. No, we don't have to unsubscribe from this often-vital modern may of communicating altogether, but we must reevaluate our approach to how we value ourselves. If you feel deeply better about yourself when a photo you upload or a funny comment you share gets a lot of likes - this can become harmful. You become slowly addicted to the little highs you get with every dopamine-boosting notification, so much so that when they don't come in as you hope, you may feel that your self-worth has also run short.

Self-confidence Through Learning and Growing

Building true self-confidence means taking small steps that leave a lasting sense of accomplishment within yourself. If you've ever learned a language, reached a fitness goal, mastered a skill, or overcome any setback to get to where you wanted to be, you will know what I'm talking about. Because you do these things for yourself - and not merely to get the attention or thumbs-up (whether physically, metaphorically or indeed, digitally!) from your peers.

If you think back to any of your key accomplishments in life, you'll likely find that it took a lot of perseverance. If you could triumph through adversity then, it's only logical for me to suggest that you can do it again (and again) in other areas of your life.

As your self-confidence grows, you'll find yourself more driven to grow with it by pushing your limits and expanding your ambitions, setting your fears of failure ، one side to make room for your hope for success. On top of all that, self-confidence provides you with the skills and coping mechanisms to handle failure. Self-confidence doesn't mean you won't sometimes face failures. However, thanks to the inner-strength you will cultivate, you will be able to choose to learn and grow from your setbacks instead of feeling crippled by them, and letting them define your self-worth, or take away your baseline of self-esteem.

Trust me - as you keep pushing yourself to try new things, you'll start to truly understand how failure and mistakes lead to personal growth. You will reach content and comforting acceptance that failure is simply a part of life: it doesn't suggest anything negative about you, but merely proves that you are pushing yourself. Paradoxically, by being more ready to fail, you'll actually succeed more — this because you're not expecting for everything to be 100 percent perfect before you act. You become less fearful to take the plunge. And it's a question of probability that the more ventures you attempt, the more successful ones you will one day have under your belt.

nfident - but not self-absorbed!

seem counterintuitive to say this, but when you have more self-confidence, you actually become less focused on yourself. Let me explain. We've all been guilty of stepping into a room and thinking, *"they are all looking at me"* or *"they are all judging me."* The truth is that, people are wrapped up in their own thoughts and concerns. When you get out of your own head, you'll be able to genuinely engage with others, focusing more on what they actually have to say, rather than what you fear they are thinking about *you*.

You'll enjoy your interactions more because you won't be so concerned about what kind of impression you're making, and you won't be comparing yourself to others. Your relaxed state will most likely put others at ease as well, helping you to establish deeper connections and come across as a much more self-assured, competent person.

Self-confidence can also breed deeper empathy for those around you. This is because when you're fully present as a result of freeing yourself from this self-conscious internal angst, you're more likely to notice the needs and subtle cues of others. When you're not preoccupied with your own self-doubt, you can be there for other people who may have their own internal struggles.

Finally, self-confidence roots you in who you really are - your "authentic self," if you will. By becoming more self-assured, you'll be able to accept your alleged weaknesses and personality quirks, knowing that they don't change your self-worth. This level of self-acceptance (more on this at the end of the chapter) is a groundbreaking step not only for your self-confidence, but also your overall self-esteem.

Self-Efficacy, Self-Esteem, and Self-Acceptance: What are they?

What about Self-Esteem?

Self-esteem is a more long-term way in which we value and perceive ourselves. It lies deeper within us than self-confidence, which can change on the hour and can be influenced by factors as trivial as how our hair is looking that day to the weather outside. This isn't to brush off self-confidence itself as trivial, of course. However, we must acknowledge its relative fluidity and openness to adapt to our transitory emotions.

Although self-esteem is also changeable, when compared to self-confidence, it is a relatively stable belief about one's overall self-worth. As such, it is more difficult than self-confidence to develop. But over time, if we build up our self-confidence, on a deeper level, our self-esteem will also be positively impacted. And due to this slow-moving and more solid nature, once built up, it is also much more resistant to what your life may throw at it. It can eventually become a grounding rock that you can rely on when times get tough, and your self-confidence fluctuates.

Our self-esteem begins to form in childhood, but can only expand to the degree that we feel valued by our parents. This is mainly due to the fact that before the age of eight, we lack the ability to formulate a clear sense of self—independent, that is, from the affirmations we receive from our guardians.

And so, if your parents didn't communicate the message that you are worthy and accepted—separate from our inevitable imperfect behaviors—you are likely conditioned to view yourself as inadequate, even today. If any parental praise depended exclusively on your actions, unfortunately, you will have the internalized belief that you are somehow *not enough*. As an unfortunate consequence, your self-esteem may be tarnished right up into adulthood.

But don't lose hope - as mentioned earlier - although building self-esteem is a long-game - it is still very much possible! And the long-term rewards are more than worth the effort.

Mainstream psychology teaches that self-esteem is made up of two distinct components: Our-self confidence, and how well we actually perform or realize our ambitions (self-efficacy). When these two boxes are ticked, and self-esteem is thus sufficiently lifted, we take the long and winding road to self-acceptance - our final glorious destination.

What on earth is Self-Efficacy?

Self-confidence is all well and good - but as just mentioned, unless you throw a healthy serving of self-efficacy into the mix - you're still going nowhere. That's because self-efficacy equates to putting yourself out there. You may learn to build up your self-confidence like a pro, but what are you going to do with all that freshly grown ego? You also have to take action to really grab life with both hands and put that self-confidence to good use.

Self-efficacy differs from self-confidence in an important way: the definition of self-confidence revolves around the ideas about your worth, while self-efficacy is rooted in your beliefs about your capabilities. In this sense, self-confidence is focused on essence and the present, while self-efficacy is based on actions and the future. And it's not much use having self-confidence if this has an expiry date, or if you aren't acting on it.

I often see clients finally make a breakthrough when it comes to how they look at themselves in the mirror every morning - they finally find the voice to speak up and the grit to seize each day. But what next? This kind of self-belief is only half-baked as this key component of self-efficacy is missing. Are you one of those people who thinks *"yeah, I guess I'm pretty competent. I can handle myself, and I acknowledge my strengths,"* only to still feel unfulfilled? To break into a cold sweat if someone asks where you plan to be in ten years time?

None of us can plan our whole lives out to every detail, and I am not implying that we should. But sticking your head in the sand at the thought of where your path is leading is only going to leave you feeling lost at some point down the line. So many of us are in denial when we think about our true desires. Are you really satisfied with your job - or are you just tired of pushing yourself for more and see staying put as the more appealing option right now? Are you truly happy drifting from one casual relationship to the next, or do you simply feel that this is better than the alternative of spending some time alone to work on yourself, or committing to someone in particular?

But this isn't just about those in "dead-end jobs" or who "can't settle down." Our paths are all our own, and I am not here to tell you that your job or relationship status are wrong in any way. This is all up to you.

These are just specific examples I often see, and you may be totally different - even in the opposite scenarios. I'm not here to judge! But it all starts with some good old self-reflection. What do you truly want out of life? It's not up to your friends, your boss, or that one family member who thinks they know what's best for you. You are an adult and you - *only you* - have authority over your own life. You would be surprised how many people need to hear that. You may even be surprised to find that you actually needed to hear it, too! Don't let the fear of judgment block you from chasing that aspiration - no matter how wild it may seem to some. People have done crazier things, I'm sure, (just think back to Thomas Edison!) and often have an interesting and fulfilling life doing so.

So many of us see the likes of the world's favorite inventors, writers, performers, and political change-makers and think *wow - aren't they really something*. And they have, of course, made outstanding achievements. Notice I say that their *achievements* are outstanding, but they are just regular people who had doubts, insecurities, and obstacles - just like you. It was their self-efficacy that they got a handle on -and this is what makes all the difference.

Self-Acceptance: The Finishing Line

But wait - here's one last very important term. Self-acceptance alludes to a more all-encompassing affirmation of the self. It requires all of the above areas of self-respect to be fulfilled.

When you're self-accepting, you're able to embrace all facets of yourself—not just the positive, more "marketable" parts. As a result, self-acceptance is unconditional and not subject to the ebbs and flows of our achievements. We can cultivate an awareness of our weaknesses or limitations, but this awareness in no way interferes with our ability to completely accept ourselves.

Everyone faces individual challenges - maybe yours are your fear of public speaking. Or maybe it's maths that's not your strong point, which makes you feel like the laughing stock of your workplace. But for everything you struggle with, I guarantee that there is a strength attached to it. If you struggle with public speaking, for example, you are probably a great listener and known for being humble and sensitive to others' emotions. (This is why it's so overwhelming when all eyes are on you). And if it's maths that sets your head in a spin, then you are likely more on the literal side - and shine brightest when given verbal or communicative tasks. Hey, we can't be naturally gifted at absolutely everything - and that's okay. We simply need to recognize our strengths and reach our flow-state to realize (in both senses of the word) our true potential, ensuring that our lives and passions are in line.

What is a "flow-state" I hear you ask? Known colloquially as being *"in the zone"* - this refers to the mental state in which a person performing a task is fully immersed in a feeling of energized focus, full involvement, and natural enjoyment. You know, when you're completely absorbed in that one activity that gives you goosebumps and makes you feel invincible? It may be painting, playing an instrument, or solving crossword puzzles - or maybe you haven't found yours yet. But once you acknowledge your core skills and passions that somehow completely immerse you and feel as natural as breathing, you learn to brush over the fact that you struggle at other things.

And this doesn't mean writing off public speaking or maths altogether! There are many challenges we must face that don't feel so natural to us - either due to professional requirements, or simply because you naturally - and rightfully - yearn to push your boundaries. Although, by definition, this isn't easy, it is a remarkably positive exercise. We all must continue to challenge ourselves throughout our lives to push our limits. But don't beat yourself up about it if it takes you a while or you fail a few times. Simply remind yourself of all of those things which you can do rather spectacularly - and that you are not defined by your struggle with this particular challenge. I stress this because while I advocate acceptance of one's "weaknesses," I still wholeheartedly encourage you to push yourself to plow on with what you find the most difficult too, safe in the knowledge that you won't take any setback to heart. The very fact that you accepted this challenge that you know isn't your strongest suit should feed your self-confidence.

And so, strive to know who you really are - what makes you tick, and what you find more testing. You'll feel more in touch with yourself and more fulfilled in everything you do - whether it falls into the former or latter category. You will have the confidence to put yourself out there when it comes to those challenges you know are in perfect alignment with your strengths. But at the same time, you will rise to challenges that lie on the opposite side of the spectrum with this newfound ambitious yet self-accepting approach.

Understanding Self Confidence: Some Final Thoughts

I regularly tell my clients that if they genuinely want to improve their self-esteem and self-confidence, they need to know what parts of themselves they have not yet felt able to accept.

The key lessons to take away from this chapter?

Ultimately, our journey to self-acceptance has many different components, which I hope you now have an improved awareness of.

No one can make you feel inferior without your consent. If you accept yourself, then that's all that matters. That is to say, it's only when we stop judging ourselves that we can secure a more positive sense of who we are. Self-confidence, and thus self-esteem, improve naturally as soon as we cease being so hard on ourselves.

And lastly, self-confidence and self-efficacy are both vital components to your self-esteem. Just as self-esteem is vital for overall self-acceptance. This pyramid-like structure of our self-worth is essential to come to terms with when it comes to not only understanding - but also learning to love and accept unconditionally - our inner self.

Training No. 1
Get to know yourself: Identifying your strengths and weaknesses

Self-confidence isn't about believing yourself to be the best at everything. The people who go around claiming that, in my experience, actually tend to be the most insecure of all. This is because their self-worth depends on what *you* think of them, so they project this seemingly perfect and confident persona. Instead of falling into that trap, try to acknowledge both your strengths and your current weaknesses.

Notice I say "current," because any weaknesses you have are simply due to a lack of training, awareness, or even interests. They aren't a permanent character flaw. You may not yet have learnt to master a skill - or never have any intention to - and that's okay. We all have skills we wish to invest time and energy into mastering - and no one can master everything anyway. It is accepting this that is the first step to truly owning your strengths and feeling confident enough to admit when you are more out of your depth - but to give it your best shot anyway!

So to get the ball rolling, I now ask you to complete the following quick exercise:

Identify 5 of your main strengths and 5 weaknesses - i.e. - 5 things that you currently struggle with or feel less confident doing.

Having it all written down should help you to acknowledge yourself as a full package, and not the two-dimensional caricature we tend to project in our professional - or even personal - lives.

Get to know yourself

Your top 5 strenghts:

○ .... ○ ....
○ .... ○ ....
                            ○ ....

Uncover your inner strenghts:

What was the most successful task or job I ever fulfilled, and what made me successful?

When faced with an overwhelming obstacle, what's my "go to" skill to overcome it?

What are the strengths that others acknowledge in me?

What skills would I like to build but have not yet had the opportunity to practice?

Your top 5 weaknesses:

○ .... ○ ....
○ .... ○ ....
○ ....

Uncover your inner weakness:

When faced with an overwhelming obstacle, what's most likely to cause me to give up?

Which weaknesses came up over and over again?

Which weaknesses might hold me back from getting where I need to go?

What are the weaknesses that others acknowledge in me?

3 weaknesses to turn into strenght :

Weakness	How to improve it	Why?
....	....	....
....	....	....
....	....	....

24

Redeem your bonus!

Hi!

Sorry for the interruption, I truly hope that you are enjoying the book.

I just wanted to tell you that purchasing "Self-confidence training" you have access to my pdf training.

I created these worksheets in pdf so you can download and print them - it is impossible to write on a screen! It will allow you to keep track of your improvements and if you need to redo them in the future.

In addition, I will send you some interesting facts and myths about self-confidence by e-mail, don't let go away this opportunity!

Well, thank you for your time and now let's pick up where we left off!

Chapter 2

Setting goals is your road to the life you want

Now that you're set with the definitions and key areas you need to improve on to achieve self-acceptance, let's delve deeper into the actions you can take to set your strengths in motion in order to get there: your goals. Goal-setting is an essential tool for motivation and self-confidence – both in personal and professional contexts. It gives meaning to your day-to-day and fortifies your activities and efforts with the intention of achieving something more.

By setting goals, we essentially lay out a roadmap of where we want to be heading in order to become the version of ourselves we aspire to be. But we must remember to include a plan of how exactly to get to that point. The more thought and detail we put into this plan, the better are our chances of achieving what we aim to.

Just Keep Swimming (By Setting Goals)

If you're one of those people who never fail to show up - whether that is to the office, the gym, or your Italian class - but fails to truly put their mind to the task at hand and challenge themselves to achieve more each day - then it could be goals that you are lacking. It takes more than just showing up to achieve the big stuff in life. You need ample motivation and determination. And this, you will find, truly flourishes when your self-confidence levels are suitably replenished.

I like to use the analogy of a shark. Hear me out!

Did you know that a shark is so heavy that if it ever stops swimming, even while it's asleep, then it sinks? This would inevitably cause issues. And so a shark never stops swimming its entire life. We can learn a thing or two from our gilled friends. If you are constantly looking towards your next milestone and nudging ever-closer towards your next goal - then you are much less likely to "sink" into that state of self-doubting apathy, many of us know only too well.

The Psychology of Goal-Setting

Goal-setting, from a psychological perspective, refers to the plan of action that we set for ourselves - either consciously or subconsciously. The E-E-E Model is a psychological approach to goal-setting that illustrates how it can affect your self-confidence and self-efficacy. In summary, it teaches that goal-setting improves overall confidence by serving three purposes:

- Enlightening Us. By providing meaningful insight into our abilities and weaknesses, and by helping us shape our goals depending on our own needs.
- Encouraging Us. By providing the motivation and courage to implement our goals to execute our plans efficiently.
- Enabling Us. Goal-setting requires us to achieve a balance between our real and ideal self. By definition, you are identifying an area of your life or abilities that have room for improvement - and taking action. And so, by setting, working towards, and ultimately achieving our goals, we regain self-awareness, self-confidence, and the ability to evaluate and take control over our achievements.

Furthermore, a pioneer in the field of goal-setting Edwin A. Locke, found that professionals in his study who had "highly ambitious" goals had a better performance and output rate than those who didn't. Essentially, this suggests that the bigger your dreams are, the more you will push yourself and thus the better you will perform. But of course, it isn't always so simple. Oftentimes we set goals for ourselves, and they are later forgotten or abandoned.

Why is it that so many of us struggle to follow through with our goals? So much so, that even the mention of "goal-setting" may now fill you with dread - as you associate it with past experiences of disappointment. Indeed, setting a goal only to fail will likely only be damaging to your level of self-confidence. So how can we become better goal-setters?

Learning to Dissect your Goals:

Goals as Easy as "ABC"

Just like when you started school, your commencement into the wonderful world of goal-setting also starts with your ABCs. There are three essential features of goal-setting to begin with, aptly called the "A-B-C" of goals. To put it simply, effective goals must be:

A - Achievable

B - Believable

C - Committed

SMART Goals

Furthermore, goal-setting as a psychological tool for increasing productivity involves five rules, known as the S-M-A-R-T criteria. *(Consider this the high school of goals, now you've passed elementary!)* George T. Doran coined this list in 1981, and it is by far one of the most popular propositions within the psychology of goals.

S-M-A-R-T goals stand for:

S (Specific) – The goal targets a particular area of functioning and focuses on building it.

M (Measurable) –The results can be measured quantitatively or at least indicated by some qualitative attributes. This helps in monitoring the development after executing the plans.

A (Achievable) – The goal is individualized and bespoke to your personal situation. It acknowledges the fact that no single rule suits all.

R (Realistic) – The goal is practical and planned in a way that makes it easy to implement into your own life.

T (Time-bound) – An component of time makes the goal more focused. It also provides a timeframe for the task achievement, making you much more likely to see it through.

Even "SMARTER" Goals

Ready to head to a higher level, still? While SMART marks the alleged golden rules of goal-setting, researchers have also since added two more elements to it, and call it the S-M-A-R-T-E-R rule.

These last two little letters carry an essential function:

E (Ethical) – The interventions and achievements follow professional and personal values.

R (Rewarding) – The end-results of the goal-setting comes with a positive recompense and brings a feeling of success to the user.

Without these last two components, your goals lack depth and may not align with your personal values and motivations. So once you ensure that your goals are "SMART," make them even smarter by asking yourself how they sit with your ethics and a personal sense of purpose.

Your Goals should Involve your Values

As such, effective goals are those, you base on high values and ethics. You must understand your own core values before embarking upon setting goals destined for success. Researches have shown that the more we align our core values and principles with our goals and aspirations, the more likely we are to feel committed to them and to then make them a reality.

Goal-Setting: Self-Confidence and Self-Efficacy

Goals play a key role in how we see ourselves and others. For example, a person who is focused and goal-oriented is likely to have a more positive approach towards life overall, as they are used to constantly looking to the future with hope and positivity. This person is fuelled by their aspirations and self-efficacy and feels self-confident as a result. They perceive any failures as the temporary setbacks they truly are, rather than evidence of inadequacy. And they keep swimming no matter what.

Tony Robbins, a world-famous motivational speaker, and coach once said that "*setting goals is the first step from turning the invisible to visible,*" and I have to agree with him on this one. Setting goals is like building doors between the present and your desired future self. The framework is built and the intention is set, but you still have to then actually open that door and walk through it. Building the door is the necessary starting point - but don't go round hammering at pieces of wood aimlessly and not following through with your intention. Instead, set manageable goals and commit to them. Otherwise, you may feel suitably busy setting the foundations for all of these possibilities - but you can't skirt over the final step - or these good intentions become obsolete.

Goals that Bind You to Reality

We become conscious of our strengths and weaknesses and choose actions that are in line with our capacities.

For example, a committed opera singer most likely doesn't aspire to open a Michelin-star restaurant, while a high-level chef doesn't usually try their luck on the stage. Neither of these hypothetical individuals are better than the other - they just have different skills and have pursued different paths. As such, it is only natural that they set different goals. The important thing is that their own goal is a fine match for their specific skills, efforts, and who they set out to be.

You may, I realize, not be so easily put into a box as an opera singer or chef. However, the need to align your skill to your goal remains the same. Perhaps it will take you a little time to figure out what your "calling" or "flow state" really is. *What will the vessel of your success and ticket to a fulfilled life be?*

However, with adequate self-reflection to identify your strengths (this, I hope you will have made some progress within the previous chapter), followed by ensuring your specific goals are "SMARTER", and you maintain the grit and commitment to them, your self-confidence will sky-rocket, and your life becomes putty in your hands. It doesn't just *happen to you* - you happen to *it*!

So look back at your strengths identified in the last chapter's exercise and incorporate these into your goal-setting. How can you incorporate these characteristics into the future you desire? Realizing our skills and accepting them is a vital aspect of goal-setting as it makes room for self-examination and helps in setting realistic expectations from ourselves.

Goals Require Self-Evaluation

Similarly, goal-setting requires you to really look at yourself - rather than only through the often cloudy lens of others' perspectives. In other words - stop viewing yourself as others may see you and instead learn to self-evaluate directly.

The successful accomplishment of goals is a clear enough indicator that we are doing well. We shouldn't yearn for validation from others on top of that. This is a commitment you make with yourself, for yourself. The fulfillment of which you only hold yourself accountable for. As such, once you reach these goals, set for the right reasons, and upon the right foundations, the satisfaction and self-confidence boost you receive will be more gratifying than any external praise.

The mastery of self-evaluation boosts self-confidence and self-efficacy - as you learn to hold yourself accountable but also to recognize your own successes - separate from anyone else's gaze. This also gives you the motivation to continue setting practical goals or yourself in all future stages of life.

Types Of Goals

All this talk of goals - but what are yours? All goals are different and require different sacrifices and efforts from you to achieve. So now let's take a look at the different types of goals you could have, to shed some light on how to approach them. There are three main types of goals:

Process Goals

Process goals strive towards the realization of plans - they focus on the steps you must take to reach your eventual goal. For example, an hour on the treadmill each morning, writing one chapter of your work-in-progress each day or reading a new book each month. Repeating the same action in a structured way like this is a process goal. The focus is the formation of a new habit that will ultimately lead to achievement.

Performance Goals

Performance-based goals are based on tracking progress and give us a reason to keep going when the going gets tough. These often come with a timeframe, for example: studying for at least 2 hours or exercising for at least 30 minutes per day can help us to regulate our efforts and thus measure our progress in manageable chunks. Maybe you want to gradually increase these efforts, or maintain this level of performance for a set period of time. Either way, these goals help you to push yourself to improve the skill in question, nudging you ever-closer to that sweet final destination.

Outcome Goals

Last but not least: outcome are goals that depend on the successful implementation of your process and performance goals. They keep your perspective in check and help you to keep your eye on the bigger picture. Examples of outcome goals could include shedding a specific amount of weight, learning a new piece on the piano, or qualifying for that promotion.

Which of these resonates most with you? Most likely, you have a combination of goals in mind at any given time. Often our goals are connected with others. Now let's take a look at some more specific and very common types of goals to look deeper into the psychology behind them.

Goals to Change a Habit

A habit is a regular or routine action, over which you feel limited control. Just as we can adopt bad habits unintentionally - such as smoking or biting your nails - we can also teach ourselves new and productive ones. Since habits are, by definition, regular in occurrence, they are relatively quick to develop - as long as you stick to them!

The timeframe required to develop a new habit or routine, depending on its complexity, is usually 3 to 6 weeks. In other words, if you persist with your habit consistently for 3 to 6 weeks, it will become second-nature to you – and thus increasingly challenging to break.

Kicking an old habit takes the same amount of time. In other words, if you don't make your 'habit' at all for a 3 to 6 week period, then after this time it should be much easier to resist, as you have broken the cycle. But kicking some habits is a little harder - such as those that include addictive substances or behaviours. Once you are addicted to something - whether it's smoking, chocolate, or checking your phone - you experience the satisfaction on a biological level. Essentially, you have rewired your own body to "need" you to continue this behavior. So don't scold yourself if you find it hard to master – you are attempting to deny yourself of what your body sees as a basic survival instinct. The key here is will-power, determination, and support.

Just remember that the result will be worth the sacrifice - no pain, no gain, so they say!

Goal to Learn a New Skill

Learning a new skill takes much longer than forming a habit. As a general rule, it takes around 1000 hours to even become "proficient" at a new skill. But this also depends on your existing abilities and where the skill fits in with those you already have. For instance, learning Portuguese is a lot easier for those who already speak Spanish.

To really master a new skill, will most likely take a lot longer than 1000 hours. However, 1000 hours of dedicated practice will give you a good grasp of the skill in question, as well as ample motivation to continue.

Outcome Goals

Outcome goals tend to take the longest time to achieve, as they involve a journey to get there. This could include becoming a partner at your firm, the headteacher at your school, or a professor in your field. Alternatively, it could be buying your dream property or writing a novel.

These goals may take years or even an entire lifetime to achieve. But don't let this make you lose heart - these goals mean you have to be in the long game, but the reward at the end will match your efforts. These aren't a quick-fix or spontaneous stab at a new challenge, but must be backed up by an entire life plan. The high level of commitment required makes it all the more important to establish early on your goal's ABCs - as well as verifying that it passes the SMARTER test.

Once all looks good, so that this lengthy process doesn't become too overwhelming, you should punctuate this journey with milestones that all work up to this eventual goal.

The Importance of Timeframe

Whatever category your goals fall under, setting realistic timeframes is a fundamental first step. How long should it take to achieve your goal? Well, how long is a piece of string? Setting a realistic timeframe depends on so many things. For instance:

Precisely what the goal is – is it just forming a new habit, or does it require learning a new skill?

Is the goal compatible with you? For instance, your intelligence preferences, behavior profile, and motivational needs, or is it going to be more complicated?

Is it a short, medium, or long-term goal? Have you tried to break down your goals into mini-goals and milestones?

What is your level of natural energy and determination?

What resources are needed? For instance, how much time, energy, or money needs to be applied to help you achieve the goal, and do you have them?

What other tasks do you have? What else in your life is currently competing for these resources? If your goal is related to your work, then it may be raising kids that divides your attention. If your goal is related to a hobby or side-hustle, then you need to take your day-job into consideration. Overall, we all must divide our resources - it is possible, as long as we are realistic and sensible in our approach.

Tips on How to Set Goals (And Achieve Them!)

Three Steps To Successful Goal-Setting

Okay, so you get why goals are so vital for your journey to self-confidence and self-acceptance. We understand the importance of timeframe, as well as their overall alignment with our skills, resources, and values. So - where to begin? How do you turn your abstract hopes into concrete goals for your own life?

Make a solid plan

The first step to successful goal-setting is a meticulous plan. Lay out your goals based on your personal strengths, aspirations, and affinities, using the guidelines offered earlier in the chapter as a base. The plan makes your new habit formation easier, as you will have already established where to focus and how to implement the actions.

Make yourself accountable

As touched upon, another essential requirement of goal-setting is accountability. We tend to perform better when someone is watching over us, so it is easier to stick on a diet or skip the gym when no one else is around. But if you learn to become your *own* severe evaluator - you can't ever hide from the observation that's pushing you to continue.

Incorporate rewards and feedback

Rewarding ourselves for our struggles and achievements makes sticking to the plan much easier. Managers who regularly implement feedback to their employees have better performance in their teams than ones who don't. And so, as though you're your own manager, you should take note of your particularly hard work or special milestones and allow yourself to feel proud. Take frequent breaks, and know when it is time to rest. Working non-stop will have the opposite effect on your long-term productivity than you may hope! You wouldn't expect someone else to work under such conditions, after all.

Your goals need to be in line with you

Remember in Chapter 1, where we explored the various areas of self-discovery, with the ultimate goal of self-acceptance? Well, when you are setting goals in your life, this self-acceptance and awareness of your every quirk is crucial. Rather than copy-pasting goals from blogs you see online or indeed, like this one - you have to specifically tailor your goals to align with your strengths, weaknesses, and specific needs and aspirations.

It's no use committing to waking up at 5 am to press weights for 2 hours before breakfast like that bodybuilder on Instagram if you have never set foot in a gym before and merely want to improve your overall health. Or deciding you want to quit all social media because your friend said it helped their mental health if for you, connecting with others online has helped you through darker times and gives you a sense of community. Everyone is different - some need to take a step back and breathe while others need to give themselves a metaphorical kick to get moving. Some of us need to be more humble and listen better to others, whereas some of us need to learn to put ourselves first and to speak up when we feel compelled to.

As mentioned before, self-confidence is all about balance, and there is more than one way to be off-kilter. There is no one-size-fits-all to become a better person - not only because we are all different to begin worth - but also because this notion of a "better person" is subjective anyway - and we all have different ideas of how we want to be.

So find your own balance. Think about what changes to your current habits may do you good and help you do better for those around you. It can be hard to look at yourself objectively in this way, but I encourage you to try. It can be very helpful to imagine what you would think of yourself from an outside perspective - how would you appear? Standoffish? Loud? Warm? Cold?

Surely, there will be some positive and some negative aspects - well, you can't change exactly how others think of you as this largely depends on their own perspectives - but you have full authority over the output you provide. And if this is the way you truly want to come across - whatever that entails - then this is a fundamental part of self-confidence - as you live out your true authentic self. You finally become your own personal manifestation of how a person should be. And this can seep through on a deeper level to impact your more stable level of self-esteem.

Focus on what you want to accomplish

We can easily become overwhelmed with our constantly accumulating inventories of tasks. One of the most effective ways to stay on top of your never-ending to-do list is to keep the bigger picture of your long-term goals in mind. Once you have a clear and overarching picture of what you want to accomplish and for what eventual purpose, you can keep referring back to these bigger picture goals as motivators. That way, if you find that your present burden isn't actually aligned with your overall bigger picture, you can stop yourself from wasting time and energy on struggles that don't form a part of this plan. Here's a great hack I like to use when there's too much on my plate, and I'm not sure where to start. Make a list of all the tasks that need to get done, and see how many of them you can cross off using the 4Ds method below:

The 4 Ds Method

Delay - Sometimes, delaying a niggling task can actually be the more efficient way to ultimately achieve your goals. It may simply free up space on your schedule for more urgent tasks, or allow you to combine this task with something related or that can be done in parallel later on. When a task isn't too time-sensitive, allowing yourself to consciously put it on the back burner can be a lifesaver for both your performance and your mental health. This isn't the same as procrastination, which is avoiding a task you know you need to do. Rather, like you are your own manager, you are deciding to prioritize something else for now, and have a plan in advance of when to start this other thing. Many cases of burnout can be prevented with this simple exercise of planning out which tasks don't actually need to be carried out right away. It helps no one to dive straight into everything as it will only make everything take longer and be of worse quality. Not only that - but you will emerge feeling so drained that it will negatively impact your next tasks too.

Delete - In some cases, delaying certain tasks in this way actually causes them to be obsolete or irrelevant by the time their allocated attention comes around. You realize that it didn't really need to be done at all - as your completion of the preceding tasks means that the item is already sorted or simply isn't even an issue anymore. This is a fantastic feeling! Not only did you manage to complete your other tasks with more precision due to your strategic delaying, but now you can actually cross off an item or two from your to-do list because the problem solved itself. Win!

Delegate - This is a tricky one as it greatly depends on what both your goal and this particular task are, your current circumstances, but also - your self-confidence. Many individuals in managerial roles need to better learn how to decide whether a task absolutely has to be done by themselves, or if it is something that can be delegated to a subordinate or colleague. Many of us see it either as a cop-out (*"I really ought to do this myself,"*), a risk (*"but what if they don't do it right?"*) or simply like an unnecessary burden (*"they probably have other things to do. I shouldn't add this to their load,"*) depending on your personality type as well as on your status and professional relationships in your workplace. But more often than not, passing on certain tasks will not only lighten your load and allow you to perform to a much higher standard with your essential items, but it will also most likely give your coworkers the sense that you trust and approve of their work, and therefore strengthening your working relationships. They may be grateful for the opportunity to try something new, or simply glad of the variety you are adding to their work. Of course, this all depends on many factors - but it's worth considering!

Diminish - This one is simply a combination of all of the above - with the end goal of diminishing your present workload, and thus improving your overall performance. Diminish your area of focus, and you will likely feel more motivated and confident about the more narrow and specialized scope of your work.

Setting Goals: Some Final Thoughts

Now you should know yourself much better - or at least be better equipped with the methods in which to start your journey of self-discovery. Your strengths and weaknesses, your short-term and long-term goals, and the different aspects of self-worth to be nourished and worked upon. So the next point is to fix your goals - to ensure that they are achievable, in alignment with your skills and values, and set within a suitable timeframe.

Goals should motivate you, strengthen your self-confidence levels, and lead to a fulfilling outcome. Reaching small goals will help you out to gain more confidence to achieve the bigger ones. Rather than becoming overwhelmed with an unrealistic stack of tasks in front of you, train yourself to use the 4Ds method in order to handle stressful situations efficiently and, wherever possible, as a team.

Training No. 2
Get started setting goals

Time for our next training exercise. I'm hoping all this talk of goals has made one or two of your own come to mind. Have you ever really sat down and actively thought about your goals - are they achievable? Are they believable? Are you committed to them?
What is the timeframe? And what resources do you need? There's no time like the present to lay all this out to get a better idea of how solid your goals are, and whether the goals themselves need extra work before you can commit to them.

Here's an example answer from yours truly to get you started:
"I would love to leave my current job and change my life; I want to go abroad and live in France
for a few years."
This is my main goal (I have IDENTIFIED the goal), and maybe I could give myself one year to achieve it. It is a goal regarding MYSELF. The problem is that, as you may know, it is usually not so easy to make such a drastic life change. There are always other goals leading up to this it.

First of all, I don't speak French - so my smaller goal would have to be to learn French so I can communicate with people when I arrive in my chosen country - and it will be easier to find a job. This time, my smaller goal is about my work: the TIMEFRAME will be 6 months. And for sure, I will need some money to buy the French course - around $1000, let's say. This, I will write in the RESOURCES box.

Get the idea? Okay, you're turn.

Get started setting goals

Divide the big goals into smaller ones! ↓

Try to find goals for every aspect of your life! ↓

Try to set a realistic and reasonable timeframe. Is it a daily, weekly or monthly goal? ↓

What do I need for reaching my goal? ↓

Identify your goal	Self, relationship or work?	Timeframe	Resources, course or training needed

Chapter 3

You can, you should, and if you're brave enough to start, you will

The most straightforward way to switch to this self-confident, self-accepting, and goal-setting master that you know is bursting to get out? Positive thinking, my friend.

A simple mindset shift can completely transform your inner-strength and capacity to cope with whatever lies ahead. So when your life becomes overwhelming, and you're not sure how to process it, remember the ever-relevant stoic mode of thinking that despite the fact you can't always control what goes on *outside* of yourself, you have complete authority over what happens within your own mind - even though it may not feel that way at times!

Trust me - you will find it a massive release to let go of your anxieties over what you simply cannot control. It may be genuinely terrible - the bad health of a loved one, a natural disaster, or a certain global health crisis...

Of course, you can't simply switch off your concern for these problems. It's not that simple - you're not a robot.

However, rather than falling into the all-too-common trap of obsessing and wallowing in the aspects outside of your control, it can be a lot less damaging - not to mention more productive - to shift your focus over to how you *can* take action.

As Epictetus put it:

"What really frightens and dismays us is not external events themselves, but the way in which we think about them. It is not things that disturb us, but our interpretation of their significance."

You may not be able to cure an illness, but you can help the person in need. You may not be able to reverse a natural disaster or solve a global crisis, but you can find ways to help your community and take positive steps to piece your life back together. Life has its challenging moments, but the key is in how you react and respond to them. This will not only give you the motivation to "keep swimming," but will give you more of a handle on your life and emotions, which will help to solidify your self-confidence as well as your self-esteem in the longer term.

Is your glass half-empty or half-full?

Although perhaps an overused analogy, how you instinctively answer this age-old question when faced with real-life scenarios says a great deal about your overall outlook on life, your attitude toward yourself, and ultimately - your self-confidence.

Positive thinking is key here - but that doesn't mean keeping your head buried in the sand! Rather, it is a question of approaching the challenges in your life in a different, more productive way. You hope for the best outcome, but you are nonetheless emotionally prepared for the worst.

For this to work, a positive inner-monologue - in other words, the way that you talk to yourself - is fundamental. If your thoughts are overwhelmingly negative, then your entire outlook on life and your own self-worth will follow suit. On the other hand, if your internal musings are more positive, your entire perception of the world and your place in it will follow suit.

If you're a self-confessed pessimist, though, you can still learn to turn your negative ruminations into more positive affirmations. The process is simple, but like all the valuable skills in life, it can take time and practice — you're implementing a new habit, after all.

How to Embrace a Growth Mindset

We all feel more positive some days than others. It would be unrealistic to expect yourself never to have negative thoughts again, or to be happy no matter what. The truth is that challenges will always lie ahead - this is unavoidable. However, by adopting an overall more positive and growth-focused mindset, you can retain a baseline of positivity no matter what turbulent times may lie ahead. By acknowledging that you will inevitably have difficult times ahead, you become less fearful. You can't control this fact, and worrying now will not make things any easier later - so you may as well enjoy every moment and tackle each issue as it comes.

Just as you must come to terms with your alleged weaknesses in skill and character to have a more fulfilling enjoyment of your strengths, the same applies to areas of your life. You shouldn't refuse to acknowledge the painful parts, but you shouldn't ruminate over them either. It takes a lot of inner-strength, but we must learn to acknowledge, accept, and move past these negative parts of our life. Ignoring negativity won't get us anywhere.

So how can you part ways with your negative, self-sabotaging behaviors and move towards a mindset of growth and positivity? Here are some pointers to get you started:

Immerse yourself in positivity

Make an effort to spend most of your precious jours with positive people who you can count on to support you and lift you up instead of dragging you down. At times, we all need to lend an ear to a suffering loved one, but overly negative people can drain your energy, motivation, and self-confidence levels while fanning the flames of stress and self-doubt. The same goes for your entertainment and content consumption: from the books and articles you read to the music you listen to — everything you expose yourself to has an impact on the overall outlook you have on your life— so take back control over this. Be conscious of what you read and watch just as who you engage with - it's for the sake of your own mental wellbeing and inner-strength.

Positive self-talk

To feed this refreshingly positive outlook, try following this one life-changing rule: *Treat yourself as you would any loved one in your life.* Be as supportive and forgiving in your internal monologues as you would towards a dear friend or relative opening up to you about a problem or mistake. And if a negative thought threatens to shake up this inner peace and self-acceptance, then consider, how would you feel if someone spoke about your best friend in that way? Defend your worth as you would somebody else's. You owe it to yourself, and your self-esteem will thank you.

Practice gratitude

Each day, make an effort to acknowledge what you have going for you and what there is to be grateful for. This simple act alone of recognizing whatever may be in your favor — be it your friendships, your family, or your current state of health — the blessings many people lest we forget, are craving. Conscious awareness of the abundance of fortune in your life in the present moment is essential for maintaining this growth mindset. Please don't succumb to the toxic temptation of only blinkering yourself towards what you *do not* yet have or what you *cannot* yet do.

Stop spiraling

Train yourself to stop and evaluate what you're thinking periodically throughout each day. If you find that you tend to assume the very worst and base your attitude on this habit, then discover ways to turn these negative thought processes on their head. Remind yourself that, come what may, you have already proven yourself to be strong and intelligent countless times, and you can face it. Whatever you may have shown outwardly in the past, you know - and only you - what you are truly capable of. You simply need the confidence to project this potential externally - and that is what you are now preparing yourself to do.

Overall, no matter what someone else may think about you, as long as you can get behind your own decisions values, you can, and will, succeed. Hold onto these affirmations internally, and you will rein in that tendency to spiral into panic at the hint of any upcoming obstacle.

Move your body

Physical exercise has been proven time and time again to elevate a persistent low mood and reduce stress levels significantly, so it's important you force yourself to move your body - even when you really don't feel like it! Once the blood and endorphins start pumping, you will feel some immediate positive effects, and it will become increasingly easier to maintain a positive mindset. But don't get me wrong - you don't have to be an athlete or bodybuilder to feel the post-exercise self-confidence boost. Whether it's just a walk in the park or a high-power work-out, the feeling that you are taking control over your body to strengthen it not only makes you feel mentally stronger, too - but it helps to shift your mindset to one of growth and energy. Exercising is perhaps the most reliable way to get an instance self-confidence boost.

Don't forget to laugh!

Lastly, give yourself permission to smile, laugh, and see the funny side - even during difficult times. Break out of that tunnel-vision feeling when something negative is on your mind. You don't have to only think about that - it won't help you or anyone else. Even if you can't avoid thinking about something completely, it's important to give your mind a well-deserved break. When you can laugh at life, it seems a whole lot less intimidating!

The Law of Attraction

You may well have heard of the law of attraction. The new phrase circulating the internet lately is receiving an intensely polarised response. Some people interpret it as a spiritual or even a supernatural phenomenon. However, for others - myself included - it is merely a concise way of explaining how life curiously seems to deliver exactly what we project for ourselves.

For instance, if you push through each day of a job you hate imagining yourself in a more desirable role, and channeling your efforts into this dream - one day, you are likely to make this aspiration a reality. But if you convince yourself that this is your fate, and there's no point pushing for anything more, then what chance do you have? Similarly, children who are consistently lifted up and told they are clever and will do great things by their parents and teachers tend to do very well at school. Fuelled by the praise and external confirmations of their competence, they see themselves as good students, and that is what they become. On the other hand, a child who is consistently told throughout their school career that they are stupid and won't achieve anything, sadly, begins to believe it. And so, this projection of themselves as an underachiever often becomes a reality.

The "Law of Attraction" essentially boils down to this: Once we believe ourselves to be failures, or that we have reached our limit and can't hope for more, we stop pushing ourselves. We stop hoping for more and become dangerously comfortable with our current less-than-satisfying reality. I'm not implying that you can have anything you want just by visualizing it, but whether you close yourself off or open up mentally to your possibilities has a profound effect on what you end up achieving.

As such, you must grasp this potential of manifesting your future. Even the most skeptical among us can see that we often end up achieving as much as we believe ourselves capable of - and this works both ways. So don't limit yourself - build yourself up! Even if only within your own mind. Picture yourself doing the job of your dreams, or living in the house you fantasize about, or in the relationship you truly want for yourself. It is only you who can deliver on these ambitions - don't make the mistake of just sitting there, waiting for what you want to come to you.

Studies have even revealed that by training your mind to focus what you want in life - but in a positive rather than self-pitying way - the brain actually, in a sense, *"rewires itself"* to strive for this ideal image, solidifying it as an essential part of your identity. As such, upon achieving the goal, you feel that sense of fulfillment you crave. If we don't, then our brain keeps nudging us until we do. Your brain has that "tough love" thing down to a tee and will hold you accountable to those goals you set for yourself.

In a way, you are creating your reality in every moment of every day. You are shaping your future with every single thought and decision. You can't take a break from it and decide not to create - because this process never stops as long as you live.

Positivity: A Question on Give-And-Take

Similarly, it often helps to project outwardly what you are searching for. Some may call it "manifesting to the universe," which is fine if you see it that way - but if that sounds a little too out-there for you, I simply see it as the give-and-take of positivity. Think about it - in nature, every single organism, from the tiniest cell in your own body to the whales in the ocean and the birds in the skies, have a sort of natural give-and-take system with the world around them. In fact, nothing in this universe is static. Every element of it - including you and I - are constantly in motion, and always giving and taking from the elements around us.

Your tissue cells, for instance, are constantly exchanging oxygen, water, and glucose with surrounding cells. On a larger scale, the earth's many ecosystems depend on the cycle of the animals eating the plants and then giving back the energy after they die and decompose. The plants take in carbon dioxide and release oxygen, while the animals do the opposite.

And so, we also flourish as human beings when a movement or exchange is taking place. We can never be completely independent of our surroundings. Try it for yourself: if you want to receive more joy, start by inspiring joy in others. If love and compassion from others are what you seek, then offer this to those around you. And if you pursue professional success, then support and celebrate the success of your colleagues. This is why selfishness and envy don't help you in the long-term. Life is a two-way street: the more you give, the more you receive.

Body language and hormones

Use Confident Body Language and Attitude

Now here is some solid advice you can incorporate immediately. Body language is one of the most powerful tools that can either make or break your self-confidence. Once you cultivate awareness for how your physical stature and non-verbal signals can influence not only how others perceive you - but how you perceive yourself - there's truly no looking back.

The science of body language can seem off-puttingly complex. But to start with the basics: in the animal kingdom, if you make yourself big, you stretch out, you take up space, you're declaring your power and confidence. And the opposite is a declaration of submission and an admission of weakness. Humans do the same thing - both as a short-term reaction to a fleeting sense of high or low self-confidence and also as a more long-term way of behaving that reflects overall self-esteem. In other words, we may all throw our hands up in the air once we win a game or cross them to our chest when we are being criticized, which reflects our temporary self-confidence - but how do you tend to hold yourself generally speaking? Are your limbs clamped shut and your spine curved, or is your body language open, your spine straight and your head held high? This is how you can get a sense of someone's self-esteem, which, as discussed back in Chapter 1 is our more permanent sense of self-worth.

This behavior is especially interesting because it shows us how universal and unavoidable our expressions of power are. You are always speaking - even when you are silent! Studies show that even those born blind will adapt to these non-verbal cues. For instance, when they cross the finish line of a race, and they've won, it doesn't matter if they've never seen anyone do this, but their arms instinctively fly up in a V-shape, and their chin lifts. It's an animalistic instinct - not just a learned behavior as we previously thought.

So use this to your advantage to change the signals you give out to the world. Imagine you are talking to an outwardly confident person - how do they look? Maybe they sit with their knees open, their palms showing, they make direct eye contact, and they think nothing of extending an arm or leg to lean nonchalantly as they talk to you. Now think of an obviously insecure person in that same chair, they probably cross their legs - maybe their arms too. Or their arms lie limply stuck to their sides, and they clasp their palms together. They avoid direct eye contact and their gaze is lowered in submission. They seem to take up as little space as possible, and their entire body seems closed off - their torso retreats as though they anticipate an attack.

When we feel vulnerable, powerless, or ashamed, we instinctively close up. We wrap ourselves up and make ourselves small. And if someone in our vicinity is asserting power, and we feel we are somehow less worthy of respect (say for example a domineering boss, an abusive partner, or if you have social anxiety, just about anyone!) we tend to make ourselves smaller as a subconscious effort to become less noticeable, and to visibly back down and submit to their alleged authority.

Well - it's about time you stopped that! Even when you are, in a sense, objectively "subordinate" - for instance, if you are conversing with a manager at work, or even at a job interview, you can train yourself to assert power through body language. You may feel small and unworthy inside, but the simple act of sitting up straight with your head held high actually takes a physiological effect on your brain, giving your self-confidence a noticeable boost. In other words - the better you are at "faking" your confidence, the more you will feel the real thing begin to emerge within you.

So think of how a self-confident person would look - how they would sit, talk, walk, or stand to wait for the bus…

and try emulating that. You'd be surprised what a difference the exterior your project can make on the inside.

So we know that our minds change our bodies, but is it also true that our bodies change our minds?

All in the Hormones

Powerful people tend to be, perhaps not surprisingly, more assertive, more optimistic, and - you guessed it - more self-confident. They're the ones who feel like they're going to win - even at games of chance. They tend to be able to think more abstractly rather than being consumed by logic. And so they take more risks. And if you were paying attention to the part on visualizing your successes, this can have a huge impact on the individual's success. It really makes you think - does optimism make you powerful, or power make you optimistic? I would argue - for the most part - the former!

That being said, there are also physiological differences regarding two main hormones: testosterone (the dominance and determination hormone) and cortisol (the stress and anxiety hormone.) Before you jump to any conclusions - both women and men do produce testosterone - but the fact that generally speaking, men produce a lot more, is considered a key factor influencing the modern phenomenon of "imposter syndrome" and the ongoing confidence deficit between males and females as early as primary school. This has a noticeable impact on women's attempts to pursue high-level roles in certain fields.

On top of that, some women produce more testosterone than others, just as some men have much higher levels than others. And studies show that the people - whatever their particular gender - who naturally produce more testosterone, tend to be more self-confident, more assertive and more competitive. The power they put out means they receive more power in return.

There is little you can do to change your testosterone levels noticeably. And high levels in women can come with other issues, anyway. But what about the part played by our gender-neutral stress hormone, cortisol? Well, power is also a lot about how you react to stress. Does anyone look for a leader that's dominant but really sensitive to stress? No - you want the person who's powerful, assertive and dominant - but not very stress reactive. The person who's laid back and takes things in their stride. The person who isn't easily frazzled or rattled and who can remain calm and collected when the going gets tough. To be this inspirational vision of calm, you must have low cortisol levels. Here's the good news: you can greatly manipulate your levels of this hormone.

Trying to lower stress levels is the best way to lower cortisol, as it is your stress and anxiety which kick your body into fight-or-flight mode. That's what gives you that heart-pounding, nauseating, muscle-tensing response before a presentation, when you just made a big work mistake, or you are rushing to get an important task done on time. Your body reads your stress as an indicator that a physical threat - such as a predator or a violent competitor - is imminent, and so it prepares the way evolution has taught it to. But this intrinsic response to stress doesn't help much in the context of our modern lives. So although cortisol may have its uses in extreme situations, when this hormone spikes too often, it can have damaging effects. You can't just fight that colleague or run away from the office screaming - and so, this nervous energy accumulated thanks to the cortisol spike goes unused. And your body is punishing you for it, jolting you into a state of terror and physical unease. It means well, though - it believes you are in the grasp of imminent death - and yet you are just sitting there still, at your computer!

By practicing more positive thinking as well as making simple lifestyle changes - such as limiting caffeine, alcohol, and sugar, spending quality time outdoors and away from technology, and getting adequate exercise, sleep, and downtime – you can effectively take action to reduce stress and keep their cortisol levels at a healthier and more manageable level.

And so, our bodies change our minds, our minds change our behavior, and our behavior can change our future.

Become a realistic optimist

Although a positive mindset is essential, it would be counterproductive to believe that hardship doesn't exist, your problems will dissolve, or that your goals will magically be achieved without you taking any action or making any sacrifice. Being a realistic optimist means an awareness of our challenges and an acknowledgment that in order to get what we want, we need to take action. We focus on the best actions to take under our specific circumstances and yet accept that which is beyond our own control. Try to combine a positive attitude with an honest evaluation of the challenges you may meet along your path. Along with imagining what it is you would like the outcome to be, imagine the steps you will take to overcome the challenges. Expect the unexpected and know that you have the inner tools to deal with unexpected challenges.

Furthermore, don't obsess over the negativity you may currently have in your life. Of course, you shouldn't ignore it either, but don't make it your all-consuming sole focus, or you'll drive yourself mad! As already discussed, a positive mindset can completely transform the way you live. You can go a step further by making use of humor to turn a negative mood or situation on its head. Admittedly, it's not always the time or the place, but I must reiterate how humor can be used to boost your self-confidence and contentment long-term. It provides you with a new and refreshing perspective about your problems and stresses, and stops you from taking yourself too seriously!

Finally, following the basics of self-care can reinforce your inner strength and completely reshape your attitude when faced with a stressful situation—for example, exercise and meditation help to release endorphins, and feed a more positive outlook. Eating and sleeping well are also fundamental for a positive mood and effective brain functioning in general! So don't discount your most basic physical needs just because the source of your stress may seem more important than your yoga class, your dinner, or your bedtime - nothing should trump these daily life rafts that keep us functioning humans at the most basic level.

Positive Thinking: Some Final Thoughts

Positive thinking can truly transform your life in the internal sense: how you perceive yourself, your self-confidence, how you present yourself to others. As a knock-on effect, it also boosts your external endeavors. Call it the "Law of Attraction" or simply a fact of life: if you convince yourself and others that you are able to do something, you will set out the necessary conditions to make it true.

If you struggle with persistent negative thinking and self-flagellating thoughts that limit your ambition and prevent you from reaching your goals, be easy on yourself - but start with this very basic practice of positive thinking. It may not seem like much in the face of all of your life's struggles. You may even find it somewhat offensive to imply you simply need to "cheer up." But that is not it at all. Positive thinking is simply a mindset shift. Although it may be a humble first step, it can eventually transform your self-confidence and self-efficacy - and this will give you that much-needed push in the direction of your goals that you are searching for.

With practice, your inner-voice will soften. It will let go of the self-criticism to make room for self-acceptance. And by becoming more empathetic and accepting of others, as a byproduct of this newfound attitude, you begin to give out into the world what you hope to reap. This can be not-only fulfilling for your own goals, but comes with the gratification that you are also supporting others on their journey to theirs.

I mean, look around — every single person you meet is facing personal challenges and struggles too. Admittedly, there is a huge range in the potential severity of people's personal struggles— but we still shouldn't forget that everyone has their particular trials and tribulations, and burdens to bear, that they face differently. You may not always see it from the outside, so be mindful of how those around you may be facing struggles not so different from your own.

Overall, whatever comes your way, when you tap into that growth mindset and the mental realm of positivity, you're better able to handle everyday stress more constructively and to look to the future with more hope, more empathy, and of course, more self-confidence.

Training No. 3
Positive Thinking and the Growth Mindset

It's time for our next training. For this one, as you may have guessed, the emphasis is on positive thinking. How can you take your existing negative thoughts and transform them with a fresh perspective?

You're out of work? Now you have the perfect opportunity to change your career path to something more in line with your strengths and ambitions. An enforced fresh start that these days are rare to come by.

You just ended a relationship? Well, it may have hurt but now all the negativity that led to the separation can stay in your past. You can now indulge in some much-needed self-reflection and work on your self-confidence as a separate entity to any other person.

You get the idea. Even your most painful of thoughts can have a silver lining if you think enough about it. Even if it is the lessons you can take from this problem, or that you will not make the same mistake again.

Well, what are you waiting for?

Positive Thinking and the Growth Mindset

On the left, write down as many automatic negative thoughts that come into your mind about yourself. When finished, take the time to challenge every negative thought by finding a positive, truthful replacement and then write it on the right side

Automatic Negative Thoughts	Positive Thought Replacement

By changing your thoughts, you will change the way you feel.

Chapter 4

Facing your fears gives you strength, courage, and confidence

Facing your fears gives you strength, courage, and confidence

One of the best ways to build self-confidence and to maintain a positive mindset through thick and thin is to accumulate and overcome challenges. Many people mistakenly believe they're confident or upbeat because of their accomplishments. However, in reality, this self-confidence and growth mindset is more a result of the obstacles they overcame to achieve these feats.

If you truly crave self-confidence, success, and fulfillment, you cannot ignore or hide away from your fears. Now is the time to train yourself to break out of your comfort zone - to face your fears and self-imposed limitations and to reach your true potential.

And here's a secret: your potential is a lot greater than you probably think. But from the cozy yet confined bubble of your comfort zone, you may not even be able to see it - let alone reach it.

What is the Comfort Zone?

There's a lot of talk these days about getting out of your comfort zone - but what does that mean exactly? You need to know what a comfort zone is in order to break out of it. And this is very different for everyone. Your comfort zone is essentially a psychological state of familiarity, ease, and control. It is within the bounds of this state where you experience low levels of anxiety and stress, where you feel comfortable and not particularly stretched, and you feel certain that you can handle whatever is on your plate. Sounds great, right?

Although I don't recommend remaining perpetually outside of the limitations of your comfort zone by constantly pushing yourself and never giving yourself a break or maintaining a steady level of effort and performance - as this can cause your anxiety levels to soar and is the reason why so many over-workers now suffer from burnout. This is essentially what happens when you don't stop pushing your limits for too long. This way, you spread yourself too thin, and your exhausted mind and body mean that you lose the spark that initiated your venture anyway. This way of working simply isn't sustainable, and if kept up for too long, you will eventually break - either physically, psychologically, or, indeed, both! You're only human after all.

But this doesn't mean you should shy away from hard work or challenges either. We're all different, and so are our particular challenges - but it's about finding that balance between stepping outside of your comfort zone to push your existing boundaries, but knowing when to rein it in, to pause, to take a break.

In the comfort zone, a steady level of performance is possible, but no more than that. In fact, many people go their whole lives, never breaking out of their comfort zone. This isn't to say that they don't overcome challenges, or that they don't achieve some level of success. But they faced obstacles as they arrived. They didn't head towards the obstacles with intent and a healthy dose of self-confidence to see them through. They achieved things that came relatively easy to them - Or put in effort but only in manageable doses - such as going to university - but only to study something that is relatively easy or connected to a stable job, rather than choosing something which drives and challenges them. Or bagging that not-too-demanding entry-level job after graduating, and then staying put there for the years that follow because it "makes sense." It's what you know. And it pays the bills. Then maybe they finally buy their own place - but in their hometown, as they never saw themself living anywhere else. Why would they? This is familiarity. This is comfort. This is just *easier*, isn't it?

I don't advocate taking the easy route either. Sometimes life just works like that. We may be lucky enough to truly want the path laid out before us and so we must grasp it. However, we all face more turbulent paths throughout life too - and we shouldn't shy away from the slightest chance of effort or difficulty in favor of the easy life. At least - not if we want to maintain a healthy level of self-confidence, self-esteem, and enthusiasm for living.

If your only obstacles in life have been a case of you taking them as they come while avoiding difficulty whenever possible, then this is living passively, my friend. If you are breaking out of your comfort zone and putting yourself out there, throwing yourself in the deep end from time to time - knowing full well that these difficulties lie ahead, but going for it anyway, then your self-confidence levels will soar. You will regain a sense of authority over your future. And I see time and time again that this completely transforms my clients' overall life successes and satisfaction.

Anxiety: Friend or Foe?

Bearing all this in mind, what can we learn from our stress and anxiety? We hear a lot of talk about anxiety these days. It can make you back away from challenges, retreat into yourself, and even physically harm your body, due to the spikes in stress hormones cortisol and adrenaline that it implies. However, did you know that humans actually maximize their performance at elevated levels of anxiety? This is known as the Yerkes-Dodson curve.

You may think this statement is in contradiction of my earlier encouragement to lower your stress and thus, your cortisol levels, but let me explain better. I stand by the fact that chronic stress is not your friend. Long-term high cortisol levels that give you that constant on-the-edge, stomach-lurching nervousness can be seriously damaging. However, as touched upon, this natural response from your body has good intentions. The spike in cortisol leads to a tunnel vision of your threat, a suppressed appetite, lowered libido, a fast heart rate, and a tensing of the muscles. This can all be rather inconvenient when you are in the throes of the average western modern life. And can't switch off from your work worries, lose interest in what used to make you happy, and feel constantly tense and sick to the stomach. But if your threat was a lion in the savannah, these sudden physical changes are what made our ancestors spring into action. The jolt of nervous energy was what gave them the strength to escape. The suppressed appetite and libido meant that their brains weren't distracted by the usual motivations of food and sex, and maintained this intense focus on the danger in question until the threat subsides.

And even today, in small bursts, we can use this anxiety to our advantage. That jittery surge you get when you're in a hurry can actually be just what you need to get the job done. That tunnel-vision feeling you get when you are determined to succeed can help fuel the fire to your success and ensure that you remain committed to your goals. You simply have to make sure that amidst all of this, you learn to switch off. You learn to leave this all-consuming drive at the office, or on the running tracks - wherever your particular breed of success is cultivated. You remember to be present when around family and friends, and to give these thoughts a rest once you are getting ready for bed. Even if you are 100% dedicated to your goal - you can't give it 24 hours of your day. You need adequate rest and downtime to get you there - so make sure that these precious moments aren't sullied by your anxiety-fuelled musings. Learn to switch them off.

So the bottom line is that anxiety has a specific purpose. When it gives the necessary burst of energy and motivation to get something done or to get out of danger - it is literally a life-saver. However, there's nothing natural about the steady stream of anxiety that many of us suffer from today. It's intended as a short term, and not a long-term response. As such, it can lead to both mental and physical health problems. So next time you get that tight-chested jittery feeling, consider why. *Where is it coming from?* And then consider if it is useful to you at this time. If you are in the last 5 minutes before an important deadline or about to cross the finish line of a race, then maybe it will give you what you need. However, if you are simply lying awake at night, socializing with friends, or carrying out non-urgent tasks - then take a deep breath. Remember that this is simply a biological response to your fears. Acknowledge these fears and move past them - however, you need to do that under the specific circumstances.

The Yerkes-Dodson Curve

As touched upon, the Yerkes-Dodson curve suggests that performance and anxiety are directly related. In simple terms, an increase in the stress hormone, cortisol - up to a certain point, of course - can help to boost your performance. Once your anxiety crosses this optimal level, though, your performance will drop pretty spectacularly. So essentially, when it comes to your stress and anxiety levels, you are walking on a knife's edge… (forgive me if this analogy only raises them!)

This idea of a curve was first proposed by psychologists Robert Yerkes and John Dillingham Dodson in 1908. In their experiment, they discovered that rats could be motivated to complete a maze with slight electrical shocks. But, as the shocks increased in power, their performance level decreased significantly, and they just ran around, seeking an escape. It was clear from the experiment that anxiety levels helped to focus attention and motivation on the task at hand, but only up until a certain point.

Next time you feel all over the place with nerves, just think of those rats. Your anxiety levels have crossed the threshold of productivity and now only serve as a biological alarm bell to get you out of harm's way, and fast. Before you continue with the task at hand, you need to take a step back and acknowledge the sensations you are feeling, and how they are actually clouding your vision and harming your performance.

Take a deep breath. You are alive, and you are a human with needs and limits. You are not in danger. You don't need to run anywhere or fight anyone. You need to remain calm and concentrate.

You can complete the task, but only once your mind is clear, your heart rate slows down, and you regain that sense of control over your thoughts and actions. It may be easier said than done, but during this journey to a more self-confident, self-accepting you, you can use this newfound sense of inner peace and security to also be accepting of your natural limitations. You can learn to push yourself when safe and necessary, but also to know when to take a step back for your own good - as well as for the good of your project. It simply takes practice and self-awareness.

Thinking vs. Doing

Hopefully, you'll remember the difference between self-confidence and self-efficacy, as discussed in the first chapter. But just to give you a quick recap: self-confidence is the belief that you *can,* while self-efficacy is the drive to ensure that you *will.* Essentially, it's all well and good to think you can achieve anything you set your mind to - but make sure you do actually "set your mind" to something at some point...

Don't be one of those people who have many plans and goals, simply doesn't follow them through, but then blames the world for it. Sometimes, things happen beyond our control, which hinder our success. Other times, our path is laid out, and the intention is there, but that lingering fear stops us from taking that first significant step. Learn to notice when you are thinking more than you are actually doing. Sometimes, we big ourselves up so much in our mind, imagining all the things we will do, that we forget the important part of actually *doing* things.

What are you afraid of? (Not a rhetorical question!)

I have found that there are three types of fear that damage my clients' self-confidence, and hold them back from achieving their potential:

The fear of Failure - "I can't do it"

If this is the fear that most resonates with you, then it's your self-belief that is the issue. As already discussed at great length, self-confidence is crucial to be able to look at yourself with a positive mindset. To believe in your own abilities, and to push yourself to rise to challenges requires for you to achieve your full potential. If you find yourself letting the defeatist mantra "I can't" invade your inner-monologue, then you must actively try to combat this. Recognise that this is an attitude, and the product of your low self-confidence - but nothing more. And remember that failures are what shape us and spur us on to do more. They shouldn't be something to be fearful of, but merely guides to lead you down the path you need to take - whether it's to try harder or try a different approach - your failures can teach you a lot about how to succeed.

The fear of Criticism - "What will other people think?"

If it's the fear of others' judgment that you find the most potent, then you are still attaching far too much importance to the opinions of those around you. You may have this issue even if you are someone with a relatively high level of self-belief - but this is too easily threatened by the slightest critique or disapproval. As mentioned in earlier chapters, you cannot live your life in fear of what others think about you. Although it's natural to care about how we present ourselves to others, many of us take this too far. We obsess so much about how we are perceived by others that we actually forget how we perceive ourselves. Even if other people truly do see you as less competent than you believe you are - as long as you believe in your own abilities, then that's all that really counts. You can change how you look at yourself, but have no direct control over how others see you. As such, your best bet is to live your life on your own terms - putting your own opinions and ideas before those of others. After all, you are your own person! And no one - no matter how well they may know you - can see the full picture. So don't let the fear of external judgment hold you back!

The fear of Rejection - "What if it's a no?"

Similarly, if you go through life afraid of the word "no" - you will really miss out. Here's the thing: the most worthwhile challenges in life are difficult. They don't come easy. And you can't be sure that you will get the result you want. But that shouldn't be enough to deter you! One "no" shouldn't send you running and hiding, as it does to so many. It shouldn't be the be-all-and-end-all. It is just one negative response - and there are always so many other opportunities out there. I guarantee that whoever your greatest role-model is - and whatever field their success was in - if they gave up after the first "no" - or even the first ten or twenty in most cases - you would not be able to enjoy their contribution to the world today.

This links back to my earlier explanation of self-efficacy - the drive that makes you turn your goal into a reality. If you are quickly put off and take any negative responses to heart, then you may not make it through the journey, However, if your self-efficacy level is high enough for you to take any setbacks on the chin and plow on forward anyway, then this is the real ticket to success. Let go of this fear of people saying "no," - it's only a short word after all - and it's over very quickly! Take this as one door shutting to allow another to open, and move on. Your future self requires it of you!

Be curious, not fearful

Be curious and realize that fear is often based on false or self-sabotaging interpretation. Think of it this way: you cannot experience fear and curiosity simultaneously. Because we cannot feel both scared and curious about something at the same time: our physiology can only be set in one mode out of the two. This means that when we switch *into* "curiosity mode," we naturally move away from fear. And since fear tends to lead us away from rational or positive thinking due to its less-than-pleasant nature, this is probably a pretty good idea...

Try this simple exercise: the next time you feel fearful about something, ask yourself, *"Is there something about this situation I could get curious about?"* Fear often comes up in situations of uncertainty, as we are hardwired to reject the unknown as a survival instinct - but as we all know, once we delve deeper, this is not always justified!

Also, consider this great quote by Bertrand Russell:

"Fear is the main source of superstition, and one of the main sources of cruelty. To conquer fear is the beginning of wisdom."

By overcoming your fears, you are not only on the path to wisdom, you are on the path to success. As already discussed in-depth, self-confidence is fundamental for success. But facing your fears is also essential for self-confidence. It's not a problem to have fears in the first place - we all do. So don't beat yourself up about the personal challenges and worries you face. Simply accept that fear is a fact of life - but so is gathering our courage to face them.

Another thing I want to point out: fear causes inaction. When I find myself procrastinating, I always ask, "What am I afraid of?" and there is *always* something deep-rooted. You may think you are just *really into* that TV series, or simply needed to clean your entire house before attempting the task at hand. But beneath all that naive reasoning, I guarantee you are shrouding a fear somewhere. You may not even realise it yourself. You may truly believe that your reasons for procrastinating are simply superficial. But most likely, you are scared of what will happen if you complete the task and it's bad. What if you channel your efforts into this task, like you're supposed to, and you realize you are just not good enough?

That's why, as a defense mechanism, many of us distract ourselves and put off these duties. It buys us time, but it also gives us a welcome excuse if things don't go so well.

"Ah yes, I really should have spent more time on that! That's why it wasn't my best work."

It gives you a reason for underperforming that is much easier to swallow. However, what if you put in the time and effort that you should have, and produced some truly outstanding work? I guess now, you'll never know. That really is a shame.

Once you identify the fear that's holding you back, you can acknowledge it and take action. Action cures fear, while inaction and procrastination only feeds it...

Dr. Sharon Melnick also suggested that *'...fear manifests itself as a series of "what ifs." "What if I fail?" "What if people criticize me and my ideas?" "What if people reject me?"...'*

According to Dr. Melnick's findings, these "what ifs" hold you back by preventing you from testing your comfort zone. She says, however, that these fleeting fears stop successful people. She wrote:

"Fear is a natural, evolutionary based response to new situations, but what ifs come from your lack of confidence

and lack of self-trust. If you don't trust yourself to be able to learn and course-correct from any mistakes, if you don't have a secure feeling that 'no matter what happens, I will make a good situation out of it', *and if you don't have a strong and accurate appreciation of your own value, then you will feel a need to maintain tight control over and pre-forecast the outcomes of any new step...The most successful people, follow the cliché,* feel the fear and do it anyway,' *because they have core confidence underneath their fear."*

Just as you shouldn't let success go to your head, you also shouldn't allow failure stop you from trying again. Appreciate your little victories and reap motivation from them. Then learn from your small failures along the way. *How can you do better? How will it be different next time now knowing what you know?* Use those pesky "what ifs" to develop contingency plans, rather than allowing them to stop you in your tracks. And don't focus on what other people think. Instead, focus on your own ideas of how you can improve, learn, grow, and make *yourself* proud. Have faith in your abilities, and don't let the fear of what may be come to get in the way of your plans.

Face Your Fears and Gain Self-Confidence: Some Final Thoughts

So that's my take on how facing your fears and taking the appropriate action can build your self-confidence and empower you to achieve your full potential. But everyone has different fears, different goals, and different capacities - so now it's over to you to figure all of yours out.

Training No. 4
Face Your Fears

It can be surprisingly hard to identify your fears in black and white. However, the most helpful thing in overcoming your fears is to become aware of them. Identify them. See them for what they are. Fear is simply an emotion or feeling that we feel based on the belief that we are in danger. Some fear is healthy such as the fear that comes from seeing a rattlesnake, as this fear will prompt you to not go near it. This is rational fear. This is your survival instinct kicking in.

However, there are other types of fear that, simply put, are completely irrational and don't really serve a purpose. They are merely based on some sort of programming, false belief system, or past traumatic experience.

Some fears are more subtle and harder to detect - such as the fear of failure, rejection, or loneliness. These are fears that you have to dig a little bit deeper to uncover. However, whether our fears are subtle or obvious, most of them are irrational and we experience them on a REGULAR basis. So if you have some crazy fears, please don't be ashamed of yourself and know that we all have them. Some of us are just better than others at hiding it.

I'm a strong believer that the right questions can help you find the right answers. So I have prepared you some questions to answer to unveil your fears and try to overwhelm them.

The first section is about detecting your major fears. You will need to have your goal or goals in mind and unveil the fear that doesn't allow you to go further and then you have to fill the deep motivation of this fear, you might need a little bit more of time for this column. Then, you need to know if these fears are realistic, you can do that by knowing your feelings when facing the fear.

The second part of the exercise is about winning the fears and what you think about fears now that you achieved your goal.

Face Your Fears

Which fear limits your ability to pursue your goals?

Goal	Fear	deep motivation
....	....	....
....	....	....
....	....	....

For each of your fears, try to see if it's realistic.
Does this fear make sense?
Is it rational?
Is it logical?
Is it true?

Take in mind just one fear and answer at the following questions:

How would you act differently if you were overcome this fear and focus on what matters?

Which thoughts and feelings do you have when faced with this fear?

○ .... ○ ....
○ .... ○ ....

~~~~~~~~~~~~~~~~~~~~~~~~~~~~~

It is time to act!

1 - Make a list of six small things you could do to face it up, from the easiset to the hardest

○ ....
○ ....
○ ....
○ ....
○ ....
○ ....

2 - Achieve these steps!

3 - Once you have achieved them, will it change your ability to manage and look at this fear in the future?

[yes] [no] If yes, how? ....

Chapter 5
Take action and get to know yourself better

True self-confidence comes from knowing and accepting yourself - including any weaknesses and insecurities - on a deep level. But how do you truly know yourself? How do you know what is actually *you*, and what is just a reflection of the expectations people have of you?

Are you really that dull maths teacher that only wears shades of brown and speaks in monotone - or is this the path you fell into to meet expectations, meanwhile suppressing your self-expression in order to fit snugly within the mold where you put yourself? Are you really the perfectly primped party girl you project on Saturday nights or via your social media profiles, or is this a two-dimensional persona you created to feel accepted and popular, while your true passions and goals are suppressed to make way for this full-time facade?

Don't sit back and let this front you put up define you, or not only will the world never see the real you, but neither will you! Just because you think that your passion doesn't fit in with the pre-existing persona, you have built for yourself - for instance, if you're that maths teacher but actually dreams of acting on stage, or the on-fleek party girl whose true passion is to write comic books. You can't live your life as a stereotype, aligning yourself 100% with an existing trope. You can still be that maths teacher or that party girl - but you can combine this side of yourself with acting out your wildest aspirations that may shock the people in your life to learn, then you are on the road to fully knowing and accepting yourself as the full and oftentimes random package that you are.

This decision to act out your goals, no matter what others may think, will not only reveal your potential but will also take you down a journey of self-discovery. You must get the ball rolling and lean towards whatever is pulling you in - or it will only tease you for the rest of your life - plaguing you with a soul-destroying stream of "what if" s.

That first leap into action

Once you have fixed your goals, thanks to the previous chapters, you can now start to take action. Sure, it may seem a bit off-putting at best and terrifying at worst. But after having done whatever you fear a few to a dozen times or so, you may think: *'Is this it? Is this what I kept putting off for so long?"*

You may almost feel disappointed with this apparent anti-climax after such a long and arduous climb to the top. You may even get a little angry with yourself and wonder why you avoided doing it for so long if it was apparently not such a big deal after all. But contrary to what you may be feeling, this was a big deal. The action itself may be small - especially that first step - but the psychological leap it took to get you there was huge. Now that you have opened the tap and felt that first trickle, the rest should come gushing. You are now ready to take action in your new norm.

Self-confidence can diminish over time if you don't hone and sharpen your skills, if you hit setbacks and don't approach them in a healthy way, or if you don't set out to take action on the regular. Even as you become more self-confident and notice positive changes in yourself, you should still continue to practise your skills to maintain and boost your self-confidence even more. You won't wake up one morning and think - "*wow, I made it, I achieved self-confidence.*" It's a never-ending journey, I'm afraid! This is why constant action on your part is essential. It's all well and good to basque in your newfound sense of self-confidence, but that high will wear off pretty quick if you don't make the most of this shiny new mindset and put yourself to work!

You can visualize and practice positive thinking all you want, but until you step up and actually prove to yourself what you're capable of, then your journey to self-confidence is not yet complete. Consider this quote:

"One important key to success is self-confidence. An important key to self-confidence is preparation." — Arthur Ashe

So now that we're on the same page when it comes to taking action, where do you even begin?

Setting Intentions

Setting intentions can vastly improve your self-confidence and dedication to your goals. Intentions are the fuel to your aspirations and the framework of your motivation. In the short-term, setting intentions can help you get a grip on negative thought-spiraling to cultivate a more positive way of thinking. And in the long-term, setting intentions may be that final step you need to take to achieve self-confidence

The most common example of how setting intentions can trigger concrete results is the placebo effect. You may have heard of it: this is when the *belief* that you will experience something causes you to genuinely experience it. In some clinical research studies, sugar pills have the same effect as aspirin simply because the participants *believe* they are getting the pain-killing medication, and so expect that their pain will be numbed. As a result, they really do feel relief from their suffering. Similarly, people can act as though they are intoxicated after drinking non-alcoholic drinks, simply because they believe it to contain alcohol. Maybe you've experienced it yourself - have you ever felt specific side-effects immediately after reading them on the bottle? Or have a go-to remedy that, although you know isn't science-based, due to the positive associations you have with it, seems to cure any ailment anyway? Hey, if it does the job...

As touched upon in the earlier section on "The Law of Attraction," these kinds of instances really make you think how simply imagining or believing something can somehow summon it into existence. In the same way, your expectations of how you will feel after taking aspirin or drinking a cocktail can shape your experience, expectations of how you will perform in an exam or a race can also have a profound impact on the actual result.

Setting intentions also gives you a feeling of inner strength to deal with tough times. As discussed, positive thinking really is transformative for your entire outlook on life. Replacing self-flagellating thoughts with positive affirmations and reminding yourself that your self-worth isn't affected by any failures, setbacks, or negative comments from others - can reduce your anxiety, make you feel more capable, and ultimately, more self-confident. The same goes for taking action with these positive intentions in mind. Don't begin a new venture thinking "it probably won't work out anyway," "I will probably have to give up" only sets this version of events in motion. By rising to a challenge with affirmations such as "this will be a great experience," or "I am really good at this, so I know I can succeed," in mind, your outcome may well look very different.

Change your habits

We already talked about how changing your habits is always tough, since you have essentially biologically wired yourself through repetition to do things a certain way - whether that's what time you get up, lighting a cigarette on your coffee break, or staring at your phone every night before you sleep. But as already touched upon, you can use this niggling nature of habits to your advantage when it comes to adopting new, positive ones.

The promise of a reward is fundamental to successful habit-setting - whether it's something as simple as allowing you to watch an episode of your favorite show after 2 hours of solid work, or as big as planning to go on your dream holiday once you finish writing your thesis. The question you need to ask yourself is: how do you make new habits stick when your nature doesn't seem to be on your side? We went over how repetition is an important factor, but this is but one piece of the puzzle. Experts propose that in order to successfully maintain healthy habits, you simply must anticipate that you will have pitfalls. Without this realist attitude, when it comes to inevitable obstacles and setbacks that will come your way, the slightest cheat or bump in the road may just throw you. However, if you take off down the road expecting it to be bumpy, then you hold on tight, brace yourself, and will maybe even enjoy the ride!

The Habit Loop — how it can be danger and an opportunity

The Habit Loop is the neurological pattern that governs any habit. It consists of three elements: the cue (what triggers your impulse), the routine (how you carry out your habit), and finally, the reward (how you achieve satisfaction at the end). An awareness of these components and how they translate for you, personally, is key to understanding how you can replace any bad habits you may have with good ones.

Since the habit loop has a hold over your automatic responses to the stimuli in your environment, short-circuiting this cycle can be your ticket to overwriting your bad habits once and for all.

Elements of the Habit Loop:

The Cue

This part is whatever triggers your habit. In general, the cue fits into one of the following categories: your current location, the time of day, your company, or whether you're alone, your emotional state, or what you were doing immediately before.

For example, the smell of fresh ground coffee as you walk past the coffee shop each day may make you instinctively reach for your wallet to place an order. Or the nostalgic jingle of fairground music may make you crave junk food you would never normally consume. Alternatively, being around certain friends or in a party setting may make you habitually drink more alcohol than you usually would, or smoke a cigarette. And being bored or lonely may be what triggers your nail-biting. Whatever the specific cue, this is what tells the brain to go into "automatic processing" mode, as your body has learned that the response to this stimuli is to carry out the habit in question. This means that it takes some real effort to resist the satisfaction it promises, as it has essentially become second-nature to you. If you fail to complete the loop once it's started, it physically and mentally pains you. Your brain has been hardwired to expect a particular reward to follow this cue and knows exactly what it must do to get it. And yet you say *no*. Even though denying yourself from this instant pleasure hit makes you feel incomplete until this neurological request is fulfilled.

On top of that, with the plethora of stimuli bombarding you each day, isolating your bad habit's cue in order to overcome it is a challenging feat. But of course, you can do it if you set your mind to it. Try to determine what exactly is triggering your habit by keeping the below questions in mind next time that familiar urge strikes. Notice any patterns that may emerge when you ask yourself:

Where are you right now?

What time of day is it?

What's your emotional state?

Who else is with you?

What were you doing immediately before this urge struck?

The Routine

A habit's routine is the most obvious element: it's the behavior you wish to change. This could smoking, biting your nails, or

Most habits have a pretty easily identifiable routine. This is the repeated behavior that you want to change.

The Reward

It's the memory of a past reward that's the reason why your brain insists on repeating this habit loop in the first place. After a previous fulfillment of the routine, it had been flooded with happy hormones due to you succumbing to the activity provoked by the cue. Your reward provides positive reinforcement for this habit, making it more likely that you will repeat the behavior later on. Your reward could be anything, whether something tangible - like a sugar rush or a nicotine fix, to something more intangible such as the validation you get from checking your Instagram notifications, watching your favorite television series, or playing a video game.

One thing to note is that the reward may not be as obvious as you think. For instance, the reward for your daily craving for a morning latte could be just the caffeine fix; it could just as well be the heightened sense of self-worth you feel subconsciously by going into that trendy coffee shop where the music makes you feel like you're in an art-house film and they know your name and order, or even as simple as the energy boost from the calories in the milk - which you could get just as easily from an apple or banana.

Experimenting with these potential rewards is the time-consuming part of getting a hold over your habits. This means that every time you feel that familiar hard-to-resist urge to repeat your habit loop routine, just try changing it. See what happens. Change the reward to see if it gives you the same satisfaction you crave. Keep track of your mood and craving changes and test different possibilities. And each time you try out an alternative routine after 15 minutes have passed, ask yourself after if you're still craving the original reward. You may just discover that once your true craving for social interaction, a few calories, or simply a break from your computer screen has been met, the original desire dissipates. It doesn't have a hold on you anymore.

Just Keep Going

You will already know that starting a new habit is difficult, so I will spare you the spiel. But when you try to achieve the result you want right away with your maximum level of effort, you tend to only make things harder on yourself and make failure more likely.

For example, if you wish to instill the habit of exercising more regularly, you may well decide to start off by working out for just an hour or two every day. Doesn't seem excessive, right? But after a week or so, you discover that devoting a large amount of time to a whole new fitness regimen when your body or lifestyle is not yet accustomed to it, is too difficult and unrealistic to maintain. Ultimately, you give up. I'm sure that pretty much all of us have experienced a situation like this at some point. You believe yourself to be a failure because you couldn't follow through with your original plan.

But what if I told you that it was actually the plan itself that was truly to blame? As already stressed at length, you must always be realistic when setting goals, despite your impatience to go from 1 to 100 in one unsustainable swoop. If you're truly in this plan for the long-haul, then you can't expect a quick fix or an overnight transformation. Set habits you can realistically stick to in the long-term, and keep going. Little by little. A tiny push every day. You barely even notice the strain, but you improve a little bit with every practice. Then, before you know it, your progress will be more than you could have hoped for.

Habit-setting expert Leo Babauta claimed that '*actually making the habit is much more important than how much you do*,' and I simply must agree. If you want to develop the habit of exercising more, for instance, the most important thing is for you to do the exercise on a regular basis, rather than focusing too much on your performance from the get-go. You could try doing half an hour a day for two weeks - you may not manage to keep going the whole time for the first few days, but as long as you keep showing up and trying your hardest each time, you will gradually find it more manageable. And so, a new habit will form. Before long, you will start to crave the exercise on cue, as your body becomes accustomed to the practice. Big improvements start small!

But what if you just don't want to?

Let's be honest, though - sometimes, you just don't feel it. You know that you *should* be doing something, but finding the motivation to get to it can be an uphill struggle. You may have a difficult task ahead of you that just gives you the childish urge to give up and hide.

It may be the physical slog of getting started, or that the particular task in question is something that makes you particularly uncomfortable - such as a frightening phone call or writing a report you just can't seem to feel invested in. Alternatively, maybe you just had a bad day and have lost interest. We've all been there. It can be uncomfortable, emotionally and physically draining, or just plain boring. We'd much rather be doing something else, and our overworked, understimulated minds can find this terribly frustrating.

And yet, there's no getting past the fact that taking action is the only way to kickstart your ambitions into motion. But how do you push yourself to do this when much of your mind and body just doesn't want to? How do you push yourself to take action, even if you don't feel that motivation kicking in yet?

If you're anything like most of my clients (or most people in general, I'm sure!), then you tend to instinctively use self-criticism as your key motivator. In other words, you instinctively bully yourself into taking this necessary action, as it seems like the only option left. Although this may sometimes work, as there's nothing like a bit of self-loathing to then decide to further punish yourself, it's quite simply not an effective (or desirable) strategy to take. This is because it fails to nourish a healthy relationship to yourself and leads to even more problems with your self-esteem down the line.

Furthermore, research has found a link between self-criticism and "unhealthy, avoidant behavior." Think watching TV till your eyes are sore, playing video games till reality starts to glitch, or binge eating. You know you shouldn't. But why is it so *tempting*? One thing you can take away from this is that beating yourself into submission is not a practical strategy to become productive, as it triggers the natural urge within all of us to resist coercion. This is why it's also the kids with the strictest parents who act up. Our evolutionary history has conditioned us to dig our heels firmly into the ground when we feel we are being pushed against our will - something that can help strengthen your defense against competitors or bullies but also is the reason behind your stubbornness.

But what if your next adversary is actually yourself? When you are your own worst critic, this can give you the perfect excuse to do exactly the opposite of what you are leading with yourself to put your mind to. That lingering infantile and impulse-driven voice inside of you cries, *"I don't want to!"* or *"you can't make me"* - and as you may well be aware, this little voice has a great track record for getting what it wants. It takes a softer approach to see real results.

Below are six steps to help you get over the internal barriers that are stopping you from being the person you truly want to be. It all starts with some acknowledgment and awareness of some hard-to-accept truths...

Step 1: Know When to Stop

Before you can even hope for anything to change, you must acknowledge that sometimes, you just don't feel like taking action. It could be the feelings it evokes - maybe frustration, resentment, boredom - or possibly even depression. It could simply be that you are overworked and sleep or nutrient-deprived. Or it could just be a bad day for you, where you feel incapable of accomplishing anything.

When you are in this state of mind, no matter how much you would *like* to be motivated, you're quite simply, and unavoidably, *not*. There's, unfortunately, no foolproof motivation button to quickly set you in productivity mode. We are humans - not robots! And sometimes our annoyingly human emotions and unexplained moods take center stage.

Unfortunately, we often cling to our quest for "good" feelings, which can lead to a lot of trouble. When we obsessively pursue these "good" feelings, we tend to avoid any activity that could evoke difficult feelings. It's for this reason that we often avoid and postpone taking action. *(Hello procrastination, my old friend.)*

Consequently, the first step towards making yourself take action like a boss is to quit trying to feel "good" every minute of the day. Not only is this setting you up for disappointment, but it is a silly goal anyway - as without any level of hardship or difficulty, we would not even appreciate the good moments at all. So let go of your idea that you must feel 100% before you begin that task.

Although it's important to take breaks, and not lose sight of your physical and emotional boundaries, being too easy on yourself will only make it even harder to take the necessary action.

Step 2: Make Room for your Discomfort

But it's not enough to give up on your attachment to feeling good – you also need to come to a truce with your negative emotions. If not, the battle will never end... As mentioned, taking action can provoke a lot of difficult thoughts and feelings. And as long as you're still grappling with your own feelings of discomfort, you will continue struggling to finally take action.

And so, instead of regarding your negative feelings as the enemy, allow yourself to experience them. Stop trying to push them away or avoid them, and simply let them exist for a while – as they will inevitably exit the same way they came! Until you let these niggling negative emotions pass through you, they will keep on nagging at your consciousness, rattling the door to your mind. By making room for your feelings of discomfort and allowing yourself to feel bored, frustrated, angry, or whatever else, you will finally be able to face the reasons behind these emotions and stop living in fear of them. You will finally be able to experience them in order to manage them, and ultimately, to let them go.

Have you ever kept pushing off a task because it brought you such a sense of dread? But then once you eventually forced yourself to get stuck in, it wasn't nearly as difficult as you'd imagined? Well, this is often the case: it is the anticipation of a difficult task that is the worst part. The doing itself is often a breeze in comparison!

This doesn't mean, of course, that you will actually enjoy these difficult feelings. However, it does mean that your difficult feelings don't need to disappear before you can do what truly matters for you. You can let them in, let them go, and be ready for your next challenge. The sooner you allow yourself to actually feel the discomfort you fear, the faster you can start to take the action required to achieve your goals.

Step 3: Connect With Your Reasoning

That being said, there's no need to feel discomfort if it's not in the name of something necessary and worthwhile. You must keep reminding yourself of what it's all for. The trick is to figure out what truly matters to you, personally, and base your motivation on this. Why is it necessary for *you*, personally, to take action? It could be to enhance your career, improve your health, or realize a lifelong dream.

Meanwhile, try to let go of any reasons behind your motivation that come from compliance, the validation of others, or the avoidance of your own guilt or self-loathing. Instead, focus on taking action for whatever ranks highly for you. Ensure that it's a free choice, as this is the kind of reasoning that really counts. So come to terms with your own goals and values, and let these be what fuels you towards action.

Step 4: Commit to your Commitments

Now comes that oh-so-pivotal moment where you set your commitments. But what are you willing to commit to? It needn't be something huge. You can start with a simple goal, and exercise your willpower over time by gradually pushing your limits – just like you would a muscle. For instance, instead of going for a 5km swim off the bat, start by going for just 500 meters and then gradually increase each time.

Don't forget that you get to call the stops here – so make them count, but also make them realistic. What are you committing to do? When and where exactly are you committing to do it? The more specific and tailored to your own life and routine, the better.

Step 5: Take That First Step

This is the part when you really get down to it and *do something.* Now. No matter how small your first step may be. Once you set your intention in motion in the form of an action, then a big part of the work is already done. Often, it is that gaping blank page - either metaphorical or not - that convinces us that we *can't*, or that we *shouldn't*. However, once you get the ball rolling, you'll be a force to be reckoned with - trust me!

So just dive in and take that first baby step. And then do the next thing and the next... follow through with the commitments you laid out for yourself. But stay with the process. Don't let your inner critic start bossing you around or sabotaging your plans. If you begin to falter, then go back through the four steps above. You got this.

<u>Step 6: Own Your Inaction</u>

When your willpower falters, ask yourself this: *who's commanding you to take action?* It's you that is in charge here. It was your decision to push yourself in this way. Similarly, by also owning your inaction, you are owning your responsibility. Are you unhappy with your results? That's okay - you have no one to answer to, and no one to blame but yourself. There's no obligation here. It's a question of choice: *your choice.*

Once you come to terms with the fact that you're in the front seat of your own life and both your successes and failures are your own, then it can be surprisingly calming. Once you shake off this infantile mindset of "I don't want to," "you can't make me," that you're intrinsically hardwired to resist, then you can accept your own authority. And it's not such a big deal if you do decide to take a break or to change your course. Just do so with the right intentions - because this is what you believe is best for you - not simply to dodge negative feelings such as fear, laziness, or frustration.

You have the ability to choose your own plan of action - when to push forward and when to step back - based on what works best for you overall, whether your inner critic likes it or not! So just as you should own your decisions to take that mighty step forward, you also need to take back ownership over your decision to step back.

Take action: Some Final Thoughts

So there you have my six steps you must take in order to break down those self-imposed barriers holding you back and to start doing what *really* matters to you and aligns with your aspirations - despite the inevitable challenges you must face along the way. It's time to let go of the idea that you must feel good every minute of the day, and allow yourself to experience those unavoidable difficult feelings in order to overcome them.

Reflect on why taking action in your life is important to you, and commit to what exactly you will do in order to ultimately reach your goals. And lastly, when you must pause or take a step back, *own* this intentional inaction. Beating yourself into submission is not an efficient nor an appealing strategy. You shouldn't have to bully yourself in order to care.

Training No. 5
Habit loop

In this chapter, you will hopefully have understood that in order to become more self-confident, you have to start doing something!

You will start to reach your first goals by taking those little steps that will allow you to get out of your comfort zone and, overcoming the first obstacles and fears, and to set your plan in motion. Once you pass this initial phase and get your first results, you will become more and more confident in yourself, finding yourself in a sort of positive habit loop.

This is exactly what you must aim for. Make sure that the steps you have taken to overcome your fears are transformed from a rare exception to a non-stop routine. Routine can be good or bad; it depends on how and to what extent you are trapped.

For example, if you are working on a big project and you need concentration but at one point you receive a notification on your phone, your phone rings, you get distracted and curious by it, you drop your task, losing concentration for your primary focus and start to scroll your Facebook newsfeed. Guess what? This is a bad habit loop!

But then there are good loops, for example, the morning routine, the fact that you need to spend time for yourself.

In this training, we will use the law of habits and routine to our advantage, putting into practice what I have already explained to you about this mechanism. You must think deeply about a habit that you want to transform into an automatic routine. Once you have done this, try to do the exercise and practice it every day.

Habit loop

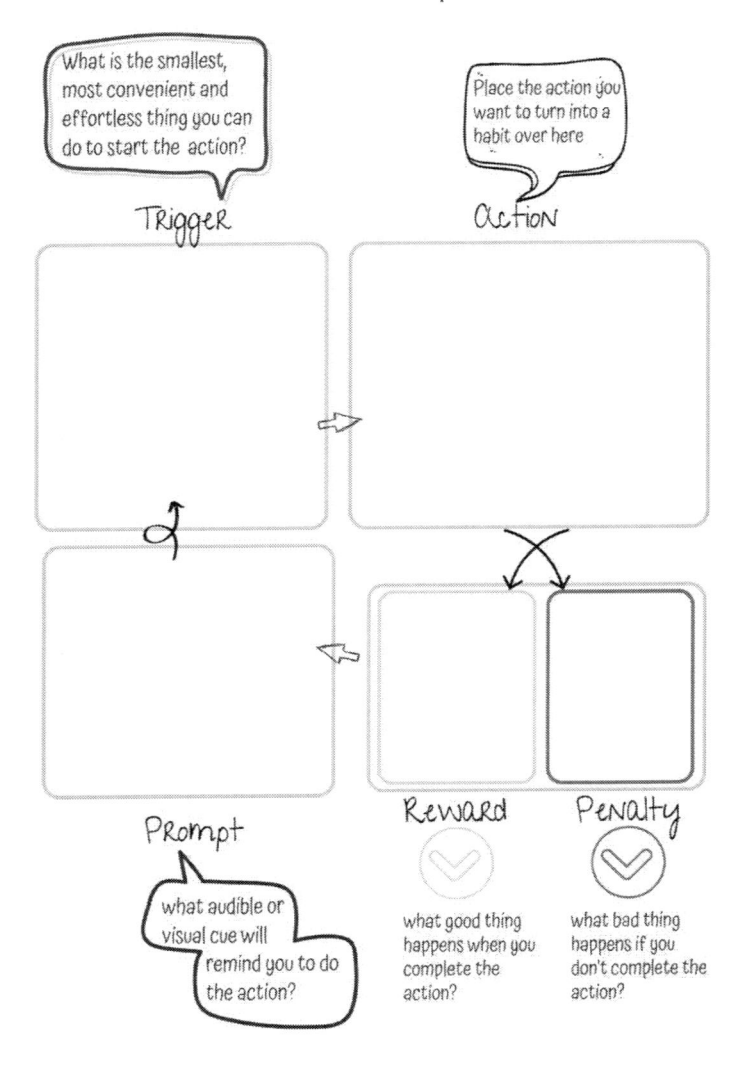

Trigger

What is the smallest, most convenient and effortless thing you can do to start the action?

Action

Place the action you want to turn into a habit over here

Prompt

what audible or visual cue will remind you to do the action?

Reward

what good thing happens when you complete the action?

Penalty

what bad thing happens if you don't complete the action?

Chapter 6

You've got to experience failure to understand that you can survive it

We have talked about owning your inactivity and not being afraid of setbacks or bumps in the road, but it can still often prove difficult to use the F word... by which I, of course, mean *failure*.

When you hear the world "failure," it may leave you with connotations of despair, humiliation, or a complete dead end. But your failures needn't feel like this! Failing in one particular route simply teaches you something - either about yourself or about the project you attempted. Is this the right project for you? If so, how could you have done it differently to achieve the desired result?

The issue is that since our earliest experiences in formal education, we have been trained to focus on getting things right first time, and to avoid making mistakes at all costs. A mistake meant an unappealing red cross - or worse still, that obnoxious "F" scrawled across your page. And so, our fear of getting it wrong starts at a very early age.

We set ourselves up for a turbulent relationship with our failures before we even go through puberty.

I propose that rather than seeing failure as a dead-end, regard it like a slight bump in the road that causes you to change course. You may slightly veer off the original path you set out for yourself when confronted with a failure, but it needn't be a complete U-turn. Before you completely abandon the mission, simply re-evaluate your route, and find an alternative way to get to your desired destination.

Still not convinced? Here are the positives you can think of the next time you fail, broken down:

Analyzing Failure

Once you experience failure and want to figure out why it happened, go beyond the more obvious or superficial reasons, and to delve deeper to understand the root cause. This requires both objectivity and enthusiasm in order to ensure that the appropriate lessons are learned and that the suitable remedies are administered.

Why do we often get this analysis part wrong? Well, I'd say it's because examining our failures in depth when all we really want to do is bury them and never look back, is quite simply rather unpleasant emotionally, and can threaten that self-confidence we tried so hard to build up.

Without adequate self-discipline and the motivation to learn from what happened, most of us will choose to avoid failure analysis altogether - maybe even deeming it the productive or confidence-preserving thing to do. Sure, it may seem like forgetting these lower moments is better for our newly fragile ego, but the longer we put off this necessary processing step, the more painful it will become when we inevitably must face up to it in the future. This is why these past failures tend to creep up on you as you try to fall asleep and let your mental guard start to slip. They have not been sufficiently processed, and so they will continue to haunt you until you can close the door on them.

And the struggle to move on from our failures is more than just emotional: it's cognitive, too. This is because we subconsciously tend to favour evidence that supports our existing beliefs instead of any alternative explanation. Another ego-preserving move we are also often guilty of when we fail is our underestimation of our own responsibility over the outcome, instead placing undue blame on external or situational factors. Worse still - we then do the opposite when assessing the failures of others—deeming them more responsible than they perhaps are. This psychological trap known as *fundamental attribution error* is prime evidence of how our flimsy, suggestible perspectives often can't be trusted at face value - and so, an objective analysis is key.

Types of Failure

Another thing to note is that not all failures were created equal. Developing an understanding of each failure's many potential causes and contexts will help you to avoid this twisted blame game, and instead implement a trusted and effective strategy to truly learn from every mistake in a constructive yet not a self-punishing way.

Our failures fall into these three overarching categories:

Preventable failures (Independent)

Failures falling under this category usually involve either an accidental or experimental deviation from the rules. For example, trying a new ingredient in your tried-and-tested cake batter that didn't turn out quite right. Or, a technical hitch in your coding due to your own human error. In this scenario, you know exactly where you went wrong. This is why I call them "preventable." Despite how it may look, I don't use this word simply to rub your nose in it that you allowed it to happen! But rather, these failures are defined by a relatively simple and easily identifiable error. Many of these "errors" were either intended as a form of experimentation, due to external factors or down to your state of wellbeing at the time (maybe you were tired or ill, which made you less sharp) - so don't beat yourself up about it! And although this makes it all the more annoying, it also makes it much easier to learn from, as you know exactly what to change for future attempts.

Unavoidable Failures (Blameless)

Then there are plenty of failures where what went wrong is much more tricky to pinpoint. They may be due to the inherent uncertainty behind the work - for instance, if you fail on a big project, you weren't well prepared for, and there were countless things you could have improved on along the way. It could also be a failure due to a very specific and unpredictable combination of requirements, obstacles, or setbacks that came along the way. Think the teams of doctors in an accident and emergency department - they may not always save the patient - but this was most likely not their fault. Maybe the patient had undiagnosed complications, maybe the doctor didn't have the adequate supplies on time, or maybe the patient was simply untreatable. This is a failure, no doubt - but the issue had so many complexities and moving parts that the blame cannot be easily allocated. At least not at first. The same goes for failures on the battlefield of a warzone, or even keeping your new business afloat. What do all these scenarios have in common? Unpredictable situations you were not or *could not* be prepared for, and the dependence on many external outcomes.

Intelligent Failures (Trial and Error)

Failures in this category are the most likely to provide you with valuable new knowledge and potential for personal growth—which is why a professor of management at Duke University, Sim Sitkin, named them "intelligent failures." They occur when experimentation is required, and failures are to be expected. The pharmaceutical company, Eli Lilly, has held "failure parties" since the early 1990s in order to celebrate those many scientific experiments that - although intelligent by design, and well-prepared - simply fail to achieve the desired results. Although perhaps taken to the extreme here (each to their own!) it is perhaps a more widely accepted fact among the scientific community that failure needn't always be such a bad thing if you see it as a necessary and well-intentioned step closer to the successful outcome you crave. After all, countless experiments need to be carried out to make new discoveries - and not all of them will be as fruitful as hoped. But that's just part and parcel of the long game. Trial and error. Learning from past results and moving forward.

All in all, we can actually learn a lot from this scientific approach to failure in the last category and apply it to our mistakes that are far removed from the lab. Why not treat your future failed endeavors as though they were science experiments? Sure, it may not have quite hit the mark this time - but this is all a part of the process!

Why we are so Fearful of Failure

Our partially intrinsic and partially ingrained tendency to hope for the best and avoid failure at all costs can get in the way of our progress and ambition. The remedy is - quite simply - to reduce the stigma of failure. But this is easier said than done.

Have you ever felt so frightened of failing, that you ultimately decided not to try at all? Has a fear of failure caused you to belittle your own abilities to avoid the possibility of humiliation? "I'm *not good anyway.*"... "*That dream would never go anywhere.*"... sound familiar? Just imagine all of the initiatives you may have attempted if this stomach-lurching fear of failure and humiliation wasn't there to rein you back in? Sure, you may have failed some or even most of these endeavors. But what if just one of these supposedly crazy ideas turned out to be a huge success? All it takes is one positive outcome, after all - so it pays to have probability in your favor.

Many of us have probably experienced this self-sabotaging fear at one time or another. The fear of failure can be debilitating - it can cause us to be apathetic, and even cynical, as we relentlessly convince ourselves that we shouldn't take the risk. You may be afraid of failing, simply because you desire to do well. This is, for the most part, manageable - as long as you keep your self-confidence in check and are able to learn and move on from these mistakes, as discussed. However, if you really struggle to shake off your fear of failure - called "atychiphobia" in its chronic form - this runs the risk of preventing you from progressing as you hope and stands in the way of you achieving your goals.

A chronic fear of failure can be due to various factors. For instance, having critical or unsupportive parents, guardians, or teachers while growing up (look back at the first chapter's section on self-acceptance for more information on how this can affect you psychologically in the long term). A specific traumatic event from your adulthood can also be a cause: For instance, if you once gave an important presentation to a large group of people and it went very badly. It could have been any past failure that you found so humiliating or emotionally scarring that you became irrationally afraid of failing in other things as a defense mechanism to avoid these feelings in the future.

So do you have a healthy determination to succeed, or a chronic phobia of failure?

Well, do any of these signs pointing at the latter sound familiar?

A reluctance to try new things or and a lack of motivation when presented with a new task or project.

Self-sabotaging behaviour such as procrastination, excessive anxiety, or a tendency to bail on your own goals before they're complete.

Low self-confidence reflected by frequent use of negative statements along the lines of *"I'll never be good enough"* or *"what's the point in even trying?"*

Perfectionism to the point that it becomes an addictive behavior. You limit yourself to tasks that you know you'll finish with relative ease to avoid potential failure.

How Not to Be Afraid of Failure

Whether you're a part-time panicker or a full-time failure-phobe, we must all learn to accept and live with the fact that whatever we do, there is always the chance that we'll fail. Unappealing as this thought may seem, the more familiar we are with it, the less hard we will take any future failures. You will realize that failure is an inevitability, and should not be a blow to your ego or received as a sign that you should give up. Facing up to the possibility of failure and plowing on with your ideas regardless is not only a courageous and confidence-boosting move, but it basically promises a more fulfilling and satisfying life.

To summarise a few ways to reduce your fear of failure:

Analyze all potential outcomes to bust that fear of the unknown. This way - you will have already come to terms with all possible failures - including the absolute worst-case scenario - before any of them even have a chance to happen. It takes away that element of heart-sinking surprise and means you dive in with your eyes wide open.

As discussed at great length in Chapter 3, train yourself to think more positively and banish your negative inner monologue. Positive thinking is an unassumingly effective way to build your self-confidence, improve your overall outlook on life, and neutralize any self-sabotaging thoughts.

Always have a Plan B in mind. If you feel afraid of failing something, having this "Plan B" already thought out can help you to be confident in the strides you take.

You could also keep in mind an inspirational quote about success or failure and use it like a mantra. Remember it whenever a failure risks derailing your self-confidence. Here are a few of my favorites:

"Our greatest glory is not in never falling but in rising every time we fall." - Confucius

"Behind every successful man, there are a lot of unsuccessful years." - Bob Brown

"Only those who dare to fail greatly can ever achieve greatly." - Robert F. Kennedy

Learning through "Safe" Failure

According to Learning Solutions Magazine, learning through "safe" failure is essential for personal growth. The key to this is evaluating each failure you make, and ranking the consequences rationally according to their severity. It may seem like the end of the world at the moment that that job you were pining for fell through, but how much is this going to seriously impact you in the long run? Try ranking each setback from a scale of insignificant impact, moderate impact, significant impact, and finally - critical impact.

For instance, that one job application or publication submission rejection is most likely only going to inflict an insignificant impact upon your life, in the wider scheme of things. A noticeable but not life-changing financial loss may be ranked at "moderate" or "significant." But your business is collapsing, or your marriage failing may well be scored as critical.

Most likely, you will find, your failures will be in the mildest two categories. However, we all face failures with critical consequences at some point in our lives. No words I can write to you will help you to overcome these, so I won't attempt to do that. However, what I *can* offer you is reassurance that even the failures at this most unfortunate end of the spectrum can be overcome. Even when you feel like you're in the depths of despair and there seems to be no hope, if you manage to build your self-confidence enough to establish a healthy level of stable self-esteem, then come what may, you will have more emotional strength to face the inevitable failures along your personal path towards success.

The Importance of Resilience

Psychologists define resilience as our process of adapting and remaining strong in the face of significant sources of stress or trauma - such as failure. Resilience may imply our ability to brush ourselves off and bounce back from these difficult experiences and into the next challenge, as well as the profound possibility for personal growth and self-discovery.

This is because improving your emotional resilience not only helps you to survive and thrive through life's more difficult circumstances, but it will also empower you to improve your life, and grow along the way.

What Resilience Doesn't Mean

Of course, being resilient doesn't mean that a person simply will not experience difficulty or distress. As touched upon, these negative feelings are often unavoidable - and it is actually more constructive to expect and embrace such feelings to ultimately be able to recover from them and move on.

And while there are personality traits that may make some people more resilient than others, resilience isn't necessarily a personality trait in itself. Perhaps, fortunately, for most, resilience involves behaviors, thought processes, and actions that anyone is able to learn and develop.

Just like building up a muscle, increasing your level of resilience requires patience, effort, and determination. You can do this by focusing on four main components — relationships, emotional wellness, healthy mindset, and maintaining a purpose. If you hold onto these four simple areas of your life and value them sufficiently, they can empower you to withstand the tough times and learn from difficult experiences such as failure.

Connecting with others

Firstly, in terms of relationships, connecting with the understanding people in our lives - whether our friends, family, or partner - reminds us that we're not alone when our mistakes and failures threaten to tarnish our sense of self-worth and self-confidence. The pain of facing the disappointment of failure can tempt us to isolate ourselves to avoid the threat of others' judgment, but it's important to accept help and support from those who care about us. Whether you have a daily with a family member or a weekly lunch with your close friend, you must prioritize cultivating these genuine connections with the people in your life who care about you.

Emotional wellness

Don't forget to take adequate care of your body, as well as your mind, as a priority. Self-care may be a buzzword of our times, but this umbrella term encapsulates whatever personal rituals make you feel both comforted and alive. Self-care is also a crucial practice for mental health and a key component to building sufficient resilience. This is because stress is both a physical and an emotional threat - both in terms of causes and consequences. Promoting positive lifestyle factors such as ample nutrition, sleep, hydration, and exercise can strengthen both your body and your mind - due to your mental health's intimate connection with your physical health. So never push your health to the side, even during testing times! If anything, these are the times where taking care of your body and emotions are even more crucial in order to maintain that magical resilience.

Mindfulness

Being more 'mindful' is another internet buzzword that you may be tempted to brush off as pseudoscience. But mindfulness essentially means being more present - not forever having our consciousness oriented towards the future - whether that's what to cook for dinner tonight, what you're going to respond to that awkward email tomorrow, or where your career will take you five years down the road.

Although, as discussed, planning is important - both for the small stuff and the big - we also must learn how to effectively separate ourselves from this constant habit of thinking ahead to the point that we never truly experience the present. It's a tall task today's reality of smartphones meaning we are constantly plugged into a relentless global conversation, but there are various activities you can incorporate into your daily or weekly routine in order to gradually ground yourself and feel yourself again. For instance, you could try journaling, yoga, or meditation. Not only do these activities bring you some much-needed quiet, and break up your day-to-day rush, but they encourage you to remember that you are alive. Your body and mind are constantly working overdrive just to keep you functioning throughout the day. And so, you should repay them the favor - they will thank you for it!

Seek purpose

Many of us feel a sense of greater purpose when we help others. Whether this means volunteering at a homeless shelter or supporting a friend in a time of need, this enables you to develop a sense of purpose, self-worth, and all while helping others. This is a fine recipe to build your resilience and baseline self-esteem while you're at it.

Be proactive

As discussed, we must acknowledge and accept our emotions during tough and challenging moments, but it's also important during times of hardship to ask ourselves: "What can I do to make things better?" If the problems seem too overwhelming to tackle in one go, there's no shame in breaking them down into manageable pieces. Come up with a small thing you could do right away to even only slightly lighten tomorrow's load. And if you make this small effort every day for a week? A moth? Then, where will you be?

For instance, upon losing your job, you may not be able to just get it back – no matter how determined or resilient you are. However, what you can do each day is spending an hour each day developing your CV and then applying to one or two positions each day. Just this small daily commitment paves the way for huge future benefits. Taking the initiative in this way despite the unfortunate cards you've been dealt with will remind you that you can muster up some motivation and determination – even during stressful or unexpected periods of your life. This only increases your resilience to make you even more confident to rise to challenges and overcome failures in the future.

Take the opportunity for self-discovery

We often find that we grow and improve in some way as a result of a past struggle. For example, after losing a job, ending a relationship, or failing an important exam, many of us go through a dark period. We question who we really are, what we really want, and where our lives are going. This may be a painful process, but we come out the other end with a better knowledge of ourselves. We not only have evidence that we can overcome something truly difficult, but we are forced to really look at ourselves and ask ourselves some deep questions. This is all a part of self-discovery, and should not be underestimated as a great resilience-booster - even if you may not enjoy the process! In the long term, it can actually cause your self-confidence to increase, and your overall self-awareness and self-acceptance will also benefit as a result.

<u>*Embrace healthier thoughts*</u>

Remember to maintain a rational perspective. Your thought processes are key to shaping your emotions and resilience. As such, attempt to identify bouts of irrational thinking - such as a tendency to catastrophize difficulties or assume the world is out to get you because something didn't go your way - and instead shift into a more balanced and realistic outlook. When feeling overwhelmed by a challenge, remind yourself that whatever happened in the past isn't necessarily an indicator of your future. You may not be able to significantly change a stressful event, but what you *can* change is how you react to it.

<u>*Accept change*</u>

Learn to accept that changes and unexpected outcomes are a part of life. Certain goals or ideals may have to be changed - not eliminated, but replaced. Sometimes, life gets in the way of our goals, and external factors throw us off course. However, accepting when circumstances cannot be changed will allow more time and energy for you to focus on what you can take control of.

Failure: Some Final Thoughts

All being considered, you may well be thinking - *sure, big up failure all you want - it is still not something anyone strives for or wants for themselves.* And granted, it's not something that you get congratulated for, or go out to celebrate (unless you work for Eli Lilly, of course...) It's a simple fact that, for the most part, failure will lead you down a road of disappointment and grief for what could have been.

However, what we should remember above all else is that we cannot go our whole life without failure - unless, of course, you don't ever try anything at all. And in this case, you have essentially failed yourself. This is where resilience comes in - something you can work on within yourself as a sort of insurance blanket, or emotional cushion, to make any future failures that bit easier to handle.

When a door closes, not only does another door (eventually) open, but you also learn that this initial door was not yours to begin with. So why cry and moan that it has closed, when you could instead by using the time and energy to find your *actual* door?

Many of us are afraid of failing, but we mustn't let that fear become powerful enough to stop us from seizing opportunities, pursuing excitement, or hoping for more. Don't let the failure win - simply let it fuel your inner fire and drive you. In all seriousness, an irrational fear of failure can have several causes - from childhood insecurities to negative experiences during our adult lives. But regardless of the origins of our fears, it's important to realise that we always have a choice of how we respond emotionally to any external factor - which includes, of course, our failures. Often, we get upset simply because we subconsciously deem it the appropriate response - like little kids who don't cry when they first fall, as it didn't really hurt so much, but then start to well up as a reaction to the flapping adults around them. If you develop an awareness of what you really want and how you really feel, separate from the gaze of others, you can get more of a handle on your emotions and become able to keep going no matter what hiccups come along the way.

Furthermore, don't lose sight of the fact that when someone rejects you and you feel your heart start to sink, you are most likely taking their subjective opinion of you as a reflection of your entire value. Surely, this can't be right! And yet we all do it. We take that one "*no*" or *"I don't like it"* as an earth-shattering catastrophe and indisputable confirmation that we suck. Basically, we take their personal opinion of this one fragment of our abilities, and then base our whole self-worth off of it... Not only is this valuing yourself on others' opinions, but their opinions on just one tiny portion of what you actually have to offer.

Doesn't that sound ridiculous when you put it like that? Well, the core issue here is that your self-confidence isn't self generated by you as it ought to be, but is instead defined by external validation. If that is the case, then his isn't real self-confidence at all - but merely a transient sense of satisfaction based entirely on others' praise. Is this what you really want your self-esteem to be based on? Wouldn't you rather be the one in control of your own sense of self?

In the modern world of excessive materialism, performance tracking, and social media boasting, we are desperate for the reminder that failure is not the exception - it's the rule. Failure is a universal experience, but since most people aren't ready to be so loud and proud about these particular moments, we are led to believe that when we fail, there is something wrong with us. Whether that's a work-related blunder, a relationship failure, a parenting mistake, or a misjudgment in your creative endeavors - no matter what you newsfeed may suggest, *you are not alone*. You need to take advantage of what our failures can teach us, and start to see our mistakes as mere guides to lead us onto the correct path - to be acknowledged but not to be mourned!

Have the humility to admit to your mistakes, accept and own them, and then make sure that you make them count in your future projects. Build your emotional resistance with every challenge you face, and let failure be a key motivator, and not only will your fears diminish, but your self-confidence and overall success will soar.

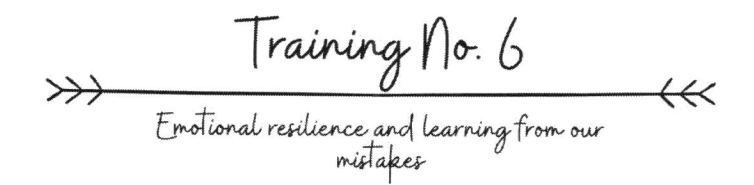

Training No. 6
Emotional resilience and learning from our mistakes

Thanks to this next exercise, you will learn to improve your ability to self-analyse, to recognise what were the mistakes that led you not fulfilling your goals, all with the intention of learning from your mistakes - which, remember, are your most excellent teachers!

Think about five difficult situations where you weren't able to achieve your goal, and for each one of them, answer the following questions.

Emotional resilience and learning from our mistakes

1. What was your goal?
Be specific; you must know what your plan was, otherwise, the first mistake you made could be the wrong goal setting.

2. What was your strategy? How did you act?
Be specific; you must know what your plan was, otherwise, the first mistake you made could be the wrong goal setting.

3. In your opinion, why you haven't achieved your goal?
Please don't blame others; try to analyse everything objectively.

4. What have you learned that will help you do better next time?
If you made a mistake, it means that fortunately, there is something to learn from it, and next time, you won't make the same mistake again.

5. What's the new plan?
Probably you need to fix something, or maybe you should try it again, and this time will definitely be better!

Stop! Stop! Stop!

Here I am again to interrupt your reading!

I just wanted to check how the book was going, but if you got this far, I would say not so bad!

Would you like to let me know your thoughts by leaving a short review on amazon.com?

It shouldn't take you too much of your time, but I assure you it would be an invaluable gift for a small writer like me.

Scan here for leaving a review!

I thank you in advance!

Chapter 7
Believe you can and you're already halfway there

So you've really been taken around the houses these last six chapters - from what self-confidence and its counterparts even mean, to how it is required to set goals, take action, and learn from your failures and to build resilience. But now, at risk of sounding like a cheesy 90's mouse mat, all I have left to say to you is this:

Once you truly believe in yourself, you're already halfway there.

It really is true - as I expressed at length in the chapter on the power of positive thinking and the "law of attraction," - if you take away one lasting message from this book, that should be it. Once you tell yourself that you can do something - or better still, that you *will* do something - the odds that it will happen suddenly soar - because that genuine intention is there. And by intention, I don't mean that throwaway *"one day, I'll do that,"* though without any commitment or the solid strategy behind it - as these are just as flimsy as they sound.

True intention can be felt within. You may not even voice it out loud, but you know that you will follow through with it, whatever it takes. Once you can visualize a clear idea of what you want to accomplish and the reasons behind it, you can begin comparing each and every task and turmoil against these overall goals and core values. And if your current activity isn't aligned with your overall purpose, then you are only needlessly depleting your energy and passion. Hey - it's better that you realize sooner rather than later!

In this final chapter, let's aim to tie the ends together of the previous pieces of advice offered earlier in the book, and complete it with a rejuvenated sense of positivity and heightened self-awareness - while grounded in the stabilizing force of realism to keep your dreams burning bright - but in a sustainable and controlled way.

Your current mindset is a result of your past

From birth, our brains are still not fully developed. This means that we're born ready and waiting to collect information from our environment and then form beliefs based on this. We then form vital neural connections that then go on to guide us via our thought processes for the rest of our lives. It's kind of amazing but also unnerving, isn't it? That so much goes on in our character development in our first year that we cannot even remember.

The beliefs we form during our childhood and early teenage years form our core beliefs right into adulthood. The experiences during these years are our most influential personality-shapers.

As already discussed right back in Chapter 1, an abused, belittled, or neglected child will form the false belief that they have less value than others because of these formative experiences. They are more likely to become an underconfident, shy, or pessimistic adult as a result of these early experiences, struggling to cultivate a strong sense of self-worth and self-belief.

For instance, a girl whose father abandoned her at a young age may form a belief that men are both some sort of hard-to-reach holy grail, but also fleeting, and untrustworthy. Therefore, she might crave male attention from adolescence but then find it very hard to trust or form an attachment to one particular guy. She might end up sabotaging every relationship to subconsciously avoid getting in too deep to only be let down, or craving the attention and approval of older, paternal men to replace this father-like energy she craved earlier on in life. Either way, this is harmful and worryingly common.

Similarly, a boy who grew up in a family where his parents always worried about money may develop financial insecurity and a strong urge to become rich. He may become very ambitious and competitive – not such a bad thing – but then suffer from depression and anxiety when these constantly increasing goals and increasingly unrealistic expectations are not met. He may remain insecure for the rest of his life about money and not having enough, to the point that he never reaches contentment or fulfillment – even if he gets to a very good place financially. This is because so often, our fears aren't based on our present circumstances, but rather, our past.

Birth order counts

But even the more mundane childhood conditions such as birth order can also have a dramatic effect on how we view ourselves and seek reassurance as adults – so none of us are exempt.

For example, the oldest child in the family may have a lot of expectations pinned on them. They will be the first child of the family to reach each milestone, and may even help out with tending to younger siblings. Meanwhile, the youngest child in a family often is allowed a little more flexibility in terms of behavior, life choices, and often showcases a delayed maturity and sense of responsibility.

Most of the projecting and pressure from parents are used up on the first child. Also, without a younger sibling to set an example for, the youngest child is usually more fun-loving and laid back then the eldest.

And so, as adults, the oldest child will likely become more of a headstrong yet sensible go-getter - always striving for the next hurdle and facing challenges head-on. This could be so, whether or not they are self-confident. Like the financially insecure guy discussed earlier, this ambition could be based on fear making it prone to crumbling. Or, this intrinsic determination could be supported by a healthy dose of self-confidence, which can be a killer combination for a successful adult to have. Meanwhile, the youngest child may grow up to be self-confident but in a different way - seeking positive experiences above all else, living in the moment, and with a more relaxed approach to life and how they achieve fulfillment. They may not have the same self-discipline as their older sibling when they grow up (thought this, of course, can be worked upon!), but the youngest child will often be a lot better at taking risks, thinking outside the box, and living in the moment.

If there is a middle child, this is the one likely to have missed out somewhat on the attention. They were not the first, not the last child, so forgo either privilege. They often fill the family role of mediator, adapting to play both with their older and younger siblings, themselves playing both the role of older and younger siblings simultaneously, and becoming a better communicator and empathizer as a result. On the downside, these are the children that often struggle to find their identity or reach self-acceptance as adults, as they spend their childhoods adapting and filling in the gaps, yet not really knowing their own place. A middle child consequently tends to thrive on meaningful relationships and making a positive difference to the lives of others, as this has essentially become their identity - something you should perhaps bear in mind if you are in this position and not sure how to achieve better life-satisfaction!

And then there are the only children, who are stereotypically the loudest and confident people - and for a good reason. Although there will no doubt be exceptions, as there are other factors too, only children from two-parent homes are often on the receiving end of the undivided attention. They grow up under the belief that they are special, unique, and with complete liberty to become whoever they wish, without siblings challenging their requests, or having to share their belongings. All of these factors - both the more subtle and the obvious differences - add up to create that "only child trope" we know so well today. But of course, although many only children grow up to be confident in that they believe in their own abilities and potential, this doesn't mean that they also develop self-efficacy or self-awareness any better than the rest of us. If anything, these two factors may suffer due to the often-stunted communication and self-discipline skills that only children cultivate. So they still have a lot to learn, just like anyone else!

Let your experiences shape and strengthen your character

Overall, we all develop certain personality traits and insecurities as a result of what went on around us as kids, from the unavoidable details about our place within the family, to experiences of trauma or feelings of abandonment. And developing an awareness of how your particular childhood made you who you are today - both the good and the less desirable - is a pivotal point in the road to self-awareness and self-acceptance.

Let this awareness of how our past has carved out our present beliefs and personality be a humbling reminder that even today, our characters are shaped around the experiences we have. Granted, this is not to such an extent as in our formative years while our brains are still wiring themselves up for the first time, but we are never immune to change and adaptation - at any age. And this should be welcome news if you are seeking self-development.

Contrary to popular belief, we can, to a certain extent, still mold our own personalities even during adulthood - provided we reach a point of self-awareness that most of us struggle to achieve without copious self-reflection and objective study of your past and present fears and desires.

So how do we go about changing our current mindset and beliefs if they become counterproductive or harmful? For instance, the belief that you are not capable or a negative mindset about your future? The first step is to become conscious of where these beliefs may have come from. Negative experiences of the past, or belittling influences in your life that have overwritten your own inner voice. Once you think you've identified the source, then you must reflect on how they may be invalid. They could be the subjective opinions of others, or a one-off event - neither of which should overshadow the beliefs you have in yourself and your life when approached in a rational way.

The forming of beliefs is an unconscious process that may explain why we feel we lack control over it. But once we take proper notice of this process and how it happens, we can grasp a degree of conscious authority over it. This is where the power lies.

Snapping Out of the Victim Mentality

Although we should be aware that our past experiences can profoundly shape who we are today, you should take caution not to slip into a self-sabotaging mindset of victimhood. The truth is that every single person has experienced a level of difficulty and hardship - both in the past and the present. Seeing yourself as a victim as a result of your personal difficulties does not necessarily mean that you have suffered from greater abuse. On a basic level, someone with a victim mentality believes that something or someone has control over what happens in their life - but of course, with an emphasis on the negative. Victims see themselves as somehow lacking in control over their own outcomes. You may - consciously or not - believe life to be against you, or that everyone else somehow has an advantage over you when you see them achieve great things.

The source of this is - once again - low self-confidence. The victim mentality is based on the belief that you are less worthy, and that any disappointment in life stems from this innate victimhood. A lack of respect and good fortune that you feel you receive. You may feel compelled to do things against your will - albeit reluctantly. You may tend to complain a lot to (or about!) those around you, as well as internally. However, you will still find yourself continuing with whatever is causing you so much anguish, falsely thinking that there is no alternative. That you have no choice in the matter other than expressing your disdain. It seems like the whole world is against you because you live passively and unhappily in this way. This is because victims always feel dependent on external forces and blame them for everything that happens. They are the ones who are always asking *"why me?"*

Even in everyday life and through trivial examples, individuals with low self-confidence may succumb to this mentality. For instance, if someone asks you a favor - to get them a cup of tea or to pick up something from the printer for them. You have your own tasks to do and don't want to oblige, and you would never feel self-assured enough to ask even a small favor like this from them. *"The audacity!"* - You scream, silently, as you jump up to fulfill their request...

And so, in this way, you internalize a great deal of anger that you *shouldn't have to* do this. That you are being taken advantage of. And yet, your lack of self-confidence prevents you from actually being assertive enough to voice these thoughts, and so you simply keep your head down and complain to someone else. Meaning that the (often, well-intentioned) asker will do so again, not thinking that you mind at all.

Everybody is tested in this way. At some point, we are all asked or expected to do things we don't feel we should have to do. The difference is that those of us with a healthy level of self-confidence will feel empowered to stand up for ourselves. We may carry out the favor, but also ask similar favors of others to show that this is a give-and-take dynamic. Or, you could politely decline: say *"sorry, I'm super busy right now, can you ask someone else?"* or *"sorry but that's not really my job,"* or whatever the particular circumstances call for.

The point is that you will read the situation and decide what you really ought to be doing, how you can be polite and kind - but not at the expense of your own dignity or wellbeing. Maybe, in reality, you *do* enjoy carrying out favors for others as it gives you a sense of purpose and ultimately is something tangible you can complain about. Or maybe it really *is* a part of your job or allocated responsibility. In which case, any internalized anger and sense of victimhood is a result of feeling undervalued or unfulfilled in yourself. Either way, something needs to be fixed.

The same stands for life's bigger situations. We are often tempted to slip into a victim mentality when things don't go our way. For instance, wallowing in the various reasons beyond your control as the sources of all your problems. "*She wouldn't go out with me because of my height,*" or "*I didn't get picked for the promotion because no one really gets me in the office.*" It can be easier on us, psychologically, to pin the blame of our disappointments on something tangible. Rather than looking at ourselves as the complex, flawed individuals that we are, we point the finger and announce a specific cause for our misfortune. This helps us to shift the responsibility of our setbacks - to berate something else, other than ourselves.

In addition to this, for many, the victim mentality can be oddly comforting. On a subliminal level, it makes us feel special and worthy of attention. Individuals struggling with this may crave the acknowledgment of their suffering from others. Because your suffering *is* real - it is simply misunderstood - even by yourself.

If this all sounds worryingly familiar, now that you have identified this obstacle to your self-belief, you can work on fixing it. To overcome your victim mentality, you have to release the negative feelings plaguing your outlook on life: fear, guilt, self-loathing, anger, self-pity. Stop pushing them away. These are the suppressed emotions that keep you enchained to this victim identity. Forgive those who have hurt you - including yourself. Reclaim the power and responsibility in your life by recognizing your own capacity to make changes. And work on changing your inner monologue as well as the vocabulary you use when speaking to others. For instance, instead of "*I can't,*" say "*I will try.*" Instead of complaining about what others have supposedly done to you to cause your present problems, focus on what you are doing now to fix them. Overall, remember that you always have a choice, and that you are no more affected by negative factors than anyone else.

Identify what needs to be fixed

So bearing in mind that your past has carved out your present - but that this goes for all of us, and doesn't make you unique - I cannot stress your need to identify your own problem areas enough. Try to see it this way: let's say your boss at work expressed disappointment at your poor performance last month. She wants you to show evidence of a marked improvement this month. However, she doesn't actually let you know why exactly she believes you underperformed, and what needs to be worked on.

Can you fix anything if you don't know what actually needs to be fixed? Of course not - you need to know precisely what went wrong in order to fix it. Did your absent father cause your abandonment insecurities? Did the fact you were the eldest child give you an impossibly high sense of responsibility and an unquenchable drive to impress? Do you suffer from a victim mentality, making you regard yourself as somehow cheated in life, and doomed to fail?

It's time to face up to the truth of your situation. It may be difficult to accept your flaws in such an objective way, but it will really help you to see yourself more clearly. Don't feel bad or embarrassed - we all have particular complexes that hold us back. But the strength and emotional maturity lie in identifying and overcoming them. In addition to that, you need to know *how* and *why* things go wrong. And the same goes for human psychology on a basic level. Unless you don't understand the underlying meaning or potential issues with your mindset or behavior, you won't know how to change them for the better.

Build your willpower

A growing body of psychological research indicates that willpower and self-discipline are essential for content and fulfilled life. Whatever cards you've been dealt in life -

we can all improve our self-discipline and willpower to improve ourselves. To delve a little deeper into this crucial element of self-care (because sometimes, like a parent to a child, we must say "no" for our wellbeing and protection...), I have selected two examples:

The "marshmallow experiment," began in the 1960s by psychologist Walter Mischel. He offered 4-year-olds the opportunity of a marshmallow now, or two if they could wait to receive them in 15 minutes. He and his team then tracked the performance of these children as they grew up. They found that children who had initially resisted temptation for the bigger reward achieved greater academic success, enjoyed better physical health, and generally had lower rates of divorce. Mischel concluded that it was this ability to delay gratification despite temptation constituted '*a protective buffer against the development of all kinds of vulnerabilities later in life.*'

In another study, 1000 children were tracked from birth right up until the age of 32. And again, the results suggested that childhood self-control went as far as to predict physical health, substance dependence, personal finances, and criminal offenses. This was true even when other factors such as personal intellect and social background were factored in. They even found that between siblings living in the same household with the same nature and nurture, the sibling with a lower level of self-control had poorer outcomes later in life, despite the identical family background and upbringing.

Overall, it is clear that the ability to resist instant gratification for a greater and yet longer-term promise of pleasure is key to our success. You can see examples of this wherever you look. From those who choose the instant pleasure of junk food in front of the television over the long-term commitment of taking care of your body - It tends to be the healthy-eater, who sacrifices certain pleasures, which achieves more long-term satisfaction with themselves over the person who succumbs to their every impulse. The same goes for the students who avoid homework for the short-term enjoyment of playing video games - they may have more fun on school nights then their studious counterparts who instead pour over their textbooks, but if the studious ones go one to get good grades and pursue successful career whereas the gamer kid fails and is stuck in an unfulfilling job, then you can see another prime example of how self-discipline really does pay off.

And the same goes for you right now - and whatever challenges you may be facing. I am sure there are countless things you'd rather do then go to the gym, study for that diploma, or stay up late completing lengthy job applications - but how would these fleeting pleasures stand in comparison to the elation you will feel upon achieving the goal on the other end of your small sacrifice?

Speaking of the gym, you are most likely already well aware that your muscles become stronger when exercised. Muscles can also be overworked, leaving them weak and sore while they recover. The same goes for your willpower. Although this means some effort may be on the cards - the good news it is, it doesn't matter where you're at right now - you can become a true willpower bodybuilder if you really put your mind to it.

Some Final Thoughts

To resume, despite the fact that we all face unique challenges in life, we mustn't let this stop us from reaching an optimal level of self-confidence. We have to overcome the tempting mentality that we are mere victims of circumstance, as though we have no authority over our own life and decisions. We must accept that no matter what previous struggles we may have faced, we have no more excuses to seize back control of our present and future.

A simple change in our self-belief and approach to our own capacity to make a change can completely transform our lives: from the goals we set for ourselves and whether or not we take action to achieve them, to how we respond and learn from our failures. For this reason, willpower is crucial - the ability to take action even if you don't feel like it, or don't feel it's fair. This mindset shift is easier to talk about than to actually implement in yourself - but it remains an essential part of any achievement.

It all starts with becoming more confident in ourselves. To not only believe that you can but to decide that you will!

If you really want to do it, you already have everything you need.

Training No. 7
Celebrate your successes

You have reached the final stage of this training.

How did you do?

This last worksheet will help you to get a handle on your personal sense of confidence, acceptance and love for yourself.

In the below worksheet, you will find a list of 15 statements and instructions.

You need to rate your belief in each one on a scale from 0 (not at all) to 10 (completely).

Once you've finished, calculate your average score.

This final score will shed light on your current overall sense of self-esteem/self-confidence on a scale from 0 (I completely dislike who I am) to 10 (I completely like who I am).

Most likely, you still have some room for improvement. So, in order to try to improve your score, respond to the following question:

What would need to change in order to move up one point on the rating scale?

For example, if you rated yourself a 5 what would need to happen for you to be at a 6?

Conclusions

You did it - you completed my self-confidence training, and you should now feel filled with a new sense of excited enthusiasm to grab your life with both hands and to propel yourself into a whole new realm of possibility now laid out for you.

Just to have a quick recap of what you should now take away from this book:

Understand your own control over your self-confidence, as well as what the less-understood but equally crucial terms of self-efficacy, self-esteem, and self-acceptance all mean.

Set goals, both for the long-term and the short-term, that are both personal to you and realistic. Learn to prioritize and strategize to make sure you follow through with your plans.

Shift to a positive mindset of growth and responsibility and banish negative, counterproductive thinking. Look after your physical and mental wellbeing in order to build the emotional strength to face life head-on.

Face up to your fears and realize that you are capable of more than you thought, and what was scaring you away from success isn't as you thought. Turn your fear of the unknown into curiosity.

Take action to kickstart those dreams into a reality and discover what you are really capable of. Seize the opportunities provided by the psychological habit loop - without falling prey to its dangers.

Embrace failure and use it as a guide and a teacher rather than a dead-end or permission to give up. Understand that failures are an inevitable part of the journey - and overcoming them an integral part of your success story.

Believe in yourself and don't use external circumstances or past experiences as an excuse - whatever your past, you got this! But remember that self-confidence is about balance and integrity.

The aim of this book was to nurture a genuine and robust belief in yourself, that you can lean on throughout the peaks and troughs of your life journey. To encourage you not to give up on your aspirations, even when they appear to be distant dreams. To have the success you crave and deserve, despite the inevitable obstacles and failed attempts, you must overcome along the way. And ultimately, to live a happy and satisfying life where you feel you can truly be yourself and feel comfortable with that.

Of course, I encourage you to refer back to the chapters covering the specific topics as they become recurrently relevant in your real-life situations. Next time you are in the market for setting goals, or seeking strength to overcome a particularly gut-wrenching failure, for example, please do have a flick back through and use this book as your own portable therapist. I trust that it can offer you some comfort and also be a source of motivation when you need it the most.

After all, we all could use a little reminder here and there how strong and capable we truly are once we lock in a mindset of positivity and growth, and are able to both acknowledge and embrace our weaknesses, fears, and failures. We must remember, above all else, that no one's life is easy or without setbacks. As such, to expect this of yours is unrealistic and only sets you up for disappointment. We shouldn't regard ourselves as invincible, but neither should we see ourselves as victims. Believing in yourself - as you will by now have gathered - is paramount when it comes to living a fulfilled life, where you feel mentally strong, capable, able to set meaningful goals for yourself, take action in spite of your fears and challenges, and overcome your failures. However, I must remind you that although I could (and often do!) sing the praises of self-confidence all day, I also can't stress enough the importance of balance. You can always have too much of a good thing.

Being overly confident - in other words, believing yourself to be *superior* to others rather than equal - leads to damaged relationships and a false belief that you are indestructible. This will only harm you in the long run. People falling into this trap may not take responsibility for their own mistakes and will push others away, or make harmful decisions as a result.

And so, we shouldn't believe our value or abilities to be inferior to everyone else's, but we also shouldn't regard ourselves as superior. Even when the success and improved self-belief starts to roll in after following the carefully curated advice between these pages, don't forget to keep yourself humble. Remember that the sustainable and constructive self-confidence that you should be aiming for is about balance. Do not overestimate yourself, but at the same time, allow yourself to feel joy due to your achievements. This will help you to put in place new targets in line with your skills - to feel pride, but also gratitude and humility.

Don't get me wrong: self-confidence is essential for personal growth and life satisfaction. It's no wonder that new books and articles on how to boost it are published every day. That being said, some authors neglect to talk about the negative side of being overconfident; I don't want to make that same mistake. It's important to clarify that extremes are always dangerous and likely to cause harm - so just as a very low level of confidence is cause for concern, a very high level is too. And swinging from one extreme to another won't help either: it's a stable, consistent, and hard-to-budge sense of inner-confidence that doesn't spike or crash, that we should be aiming for.

We may feel more confident some days than others. This is, of course, a normal part of life's fluctuations. But the goal is for your self-confidence not to vary *too much*. It should preferably always stay within a manageable and healthy window, come what may.

Overall, the resounding difference between a healthily high level of self-confidence, and an unhealthy, over-confident attitude, is that the former is the belief that you are just as capable and worthy as everyone else, whereas the latter leads you to believe that you are actually *more* capable and worthy. On the other end of the scale, if you are grappling with a victim mentality, you underestimate your capability to take action in your life. Both of these extremes are toxic and can greatly damage your relationships and success.

So get to know and believe in yourself no matter what - but recognize and believe in others too. Your journey to self-confidence and self-acceptance isn't only yours - but a universal journey we all must take.

Some Final Thoughts

I must reiterate that you already have all that is required within you to shape your life into the one you've always wanted. But you must make an effort to sharpen your existing skills, get to know yourself - flaws and all - very deeply, and to foster the self-confidence to see you through. Simply "getting by" and letting life happen to you without taking any real control over it - especially if you then use those energy conserves to complain incessantly about how things aren't going your way - is such a waste of your potential and a drain on your self-esteem.

You must now take the building blocks offered in this book to establish a healthy and balanced sense of self-confidence to make you feel equipped to face your life and your personal struggles head-on.

At the beginning of this journey, I promised you that if you overcome the self-doubt, you're currently grappling with - and you put in all the necessary effort, you will be able to reach your goals. I pledged to show you how to tap into a new realm of self-confidence to transform your passive life into an active one. Please take away the lasting message that if you live every single moment at your full capacity (while taking the necessary rest and self-care measures, of course!), then you won't have any regrets. You will be sure that you achieved your potential - you went down every avenue you wished, and you tried everything you wanted.

By now, I trust you have a deep understanding of how nurturing your self-confidence as your one true source of motivation is the key to life satisfaction of achieving success. Your self-confidence, when sustained at a healthy level, will propel you into the heights and straight through the lows. It will enable you to see clearly the perfect imperfection of life, and the inevitable twists and turns of your own. It will keep you feeling strong and capable when challenged, and positive and determined to overcome your setbacks. It will help you to present your true self to the world - not just the shy fraction of your true personality that is all you previously dared to reveal to the outside world.

You will feel more empowered. More authentic. More daring to set your bar high, set the goals you need to dive into the future you want, face up to your fears, laugh off your failures, and above all - believe in yourself no matter what.

So get to know who you really are - what you really want out of your life, and how you will take action to get it. You are your own greatest advocate if you allow yourself to be! But recognize and believe in others too. Your journey to self-confidence and self-acceptance isn't only yours - but a universal mission we all must take.

To finish with an apt quote by American author and activist, Marianne Williamson:

'Who am I to be brilliant, gorgeous, talented, fabulous?'
Actually, who are you not to be?'

Sebastian O'Brien

References:

4 D Diagnostic Tool. (n.d.). Retrieved from http://lauraleerose.com/4%20D%20Diagnostic%20Tool.pdf

A. (n.d.). 7 Ways to Give up the Victim Mentality and Live with Confidence. Retrieved from https://www.purposefairy.com/67135/7-ways-to-give-up-the-victim-mentality-and-live-with-confidence/

Adult health. (n.d.). Retrieved from https://www.mayoclinic.org/healthy-lifestyle/adult-health/in-depth/self-esteem/art-20047976

Azimy, R. (2020, March). The Power of Positive Thinking. Retrieved from https://medium.com/illumination/the-power-of-positive-thinking-88a120ae2a57

Behance, Inc. (2019, February 27). The Thinking Mindset vs. The Doing Mindset: Pick One (And Only One). Retrieved from https://99u.adobe.com/articles/7240/the-thinking-mindset-vs-the-doing-mindset-pick-one-and-only-one

Belin, A. (2020, April 22). How to Crush Your Lack of Motivation and Always Stay Motivated. Retrieved from https://www.lifehack.org/articles/communication/how-to-forever-cure-to-your-lack-of-motivation.html

Bilanich, B. (2012, July 30). Fear is the Enemy of Self Confidence. Retrieved from https://www.fastcompany.com/1084542/fear-enemy-self-confidence

Building confidence. (2020). Retrieved from https://www.skillsyouneed.com/ps/confidence.html

Changing Habits – (2020, March 16). Retrieved from https://learningcenter.unc.edu/tips-and-tools/changing-habits/

Cherry, K. (2019, July). When Too Much Self-Confidence Is a Bad Thing. Retrieved from https://www.verywellmind.com/can-you-have-too-much-self-confidence-4163364

Cuddy, A. (2010). Your body language may shape who you are. Retrieved from https://www.ted.com/talks/amy_cuddy_your_body_language_may_shape_who_you_are/transcript?language=en

Dayton, D. (2018, November). Definition of Short Term Goal Setting. Retrieved from https://careertrend.com/definition-short-term-goal-setting-36343.html

Dulin, D. (2019, June). 15 killer action steps to building self confidence. Retrieved from https://www.unfinishedsuccess.com/building-self-confidence/

Embrace the Benefits of Safe Failure. (n.d.). Retrieved from https://learningsolutionsmag.com/articles/1355/embrace-the-benefits-of-safe-failure

Galli, A. (2018, June 21). How to Be Outrageously Consistent | 7 Tips to Be Consistently Consistent. Retrieved from https://medium.com/the-mission/how-to-be-outrageously-consistent-7-tips-to-be-consistently-consistent-a32fd1c0a250

Growth Mindset: The Surprising Psychology of Self-Belief. (2019). Retrieved from https://nickwignall.com/growth-mindset/

Hayes, S. (n.d.). How To Take Action When You Don't Wanna. Retrieved from https://www.psychologytoday.com/us/blog/get-out-your-mind/201802/how-take-action-when-you-don-t-wanna

How Setting Intentions Improved My Confidence | HealthyPlace. (2015, October 9). Retrieved from https://www.healthyplace.com/blogs/buildingselfesteem/2015/10/how-setting-intentions-improved-my-confidence

How to Learn From Your Mistakes: And Put Those Lessons Into Practice. (n.d.). Retrieved from https://www.mindtools.com/pages/article/learn-from-mistakes.htm

How to maintain confidence after experiencing failure - Quora. (n.d.). Retrieved from https://www.quora.com/How-do-you-maintain-confidence-after-experiencing-failure

https://www.skillsyouneed.com/ps/confidence.html. (2020). Retrieved from https://www.skillsyouneed.com/ps/confidence.html

HuffPost is now a part of Verizon Media. (n.d.-a). Retrieved from https://www.huffpost.com/entry/embrace-your-own-reality-its-the-key-to-happiness_b_7102544

HuffPost is now a part of Verizon Media. (n.d.-b). Retrieved from https://www.huffpost.com/entry/realistic-optimist_b_8018530

I.O. (2017). 5 Reasons Why You Must Develop Your Self-Confidence. Retrieved from https://magazine.vunela.com/5-reasons-why-you-must-develop-your-self-confidence-7d69523a9c7e

Josa, C. (2018, July 27). Imposter Syndrome: It's Not All In Your Head. Retrieved from http://www.clarejosa.com/inspiration/clear-out-your-blocks/imposter-syndrome-not-head/

K.W. (2015, October). Self-Confidence and Self-Esteem Aren't the Same Thing. Retrieved from https://lifehacker.com/self-confidence-and-self-esteem-aren-t-the-same-thing-1737949859

Lesson Plan 5: Stepping Out of My Comfort Zone. (n.d.). Retrieved from http://www.successfullives.co.uk/wp-content/uploads/Teacher-Lesson-Plan-5-Stepping-Out-of-My-Comfort-Zone.pdf

Mohr, T. (2019, June 12). Bringing Curiosity to Fear. Retrieved from https://www.taramohr.com/dealing-with-fear/bring-curiosity-to-fear/

Moore, A. (n.d.). How to Activate Extreme Self-Confidence and Destroy Chronic Anxiety and Fear. Retrieved from https://thriveglobal.com/stories/how-to-activate-extreme-self-confidence-and-destroy-chronic-anxiety-and-fear/

Moran, G. (n.d.). Yes, you’ll fail. This is how you’ll actually learn from it. Retrieved from https://www.fastcompany.com/90314749/the-right-way-to-fail

Moulder, H. (n.d.). How to Set Goals for Building Self-Confidence and Fulfillment. Retrieved from https://www.coursecorrectioncoaching.com/how-to-set-goals-for-building-self-confidence-and-fulfillment/#Goals_and_Self-Confidence

Muller, D. (2020). How to remove cortisol from the body naturally. Retrieved from https://www.medicalnewstoday.com/articles/322335

Overcoming Fear of Failure: Facing Fears and Moving Forward. (n.d.). Retrieved from https://www.mindtools.com/pages/article/fear-of-failure.htm

Pflug, T. (2019, August 30). How Taking Action is Helping You Grow Your Self-Confidence. Retrieved from https://personal-development-zone.com/taking-action-self-confidence/

Seltzer Ph.D., L. F. (2010, August). The Path to Unconditional Self-Acceptance. Retrieved from https://www.psychologytoday.com/ie/blog/evolution-the-self/200809/the-path-unconditional-self-acceptance

Setting Realistic Timeframes for Goals. (n.d.). Retrieved from https://www.achieve-goal-setting-success.com/timeframes.html

Shrestha, P. (2019, June 16). Yerkes - Dodson Law. Retrieved from https://www.psychestudy.com/general/motivation-emotion/yerkes-dodson-law

SMART Goals 101. (n.d.). Retrieved from https://www.briantracy.com/blog/personal-success/smart-goals/

Steven Stosny, Ph.D. (2014, June). How Much Do You Value Yourself? Retrieved from https://www.psychologytoday.com/ie/blog/anger-in-the-age-entitlement/201406/how-much-do-you-value-yourself

Strategies for Learning from Failure. (n.d.). Retrieved from https://hbr.org/2011/04/strategies-for-learning-from-failure

The Dangers of Excessively High Self-Esteem. (2019). Retrieved from https://exploringyourmind.com/the-dangers-of-excessively-high-self-esteem/

The Habit Loop | Habitica Wiki | Fandom. (n.d.). Retrieved from https://habitica.fandom.com/wiki/The_Habit_Loop

The Science & Psychology Of Goal-Setting 101. (2020, February). Retrieved from https://positivepsychology.com/goal-setting-psychology/

Using the Law of Attraction for Joy, Relationships, Money & Success. (n.d.). Retrieved from https://www.jackcanfield.com/blog/using-the-law-of-attraction/

What is Self-Confidence? + 9 Ways to Increase It. (2020). Retrieved from https://positivepsychology.com/self-confidence/

Why Self-Confidence Is More Important Than You Think. (2018). Retrieved from https://www.psychologytoday.com/ie/blog/shyness-is-nice/201809/why-self-confidence-is-more-important-you-think

Why we should embrace failure. (n.d.). Retrieved from https://believeperform.com/why-we-should-embrace-failure/

wikiHow. (2018, September 27). How to Build Confidence by Facing Your Fears. Retrieved from https://www.wikihow.com/Build-Confidence-by-Facing-Your-Fears

Zetlin, M. (2020a, February 6). Here's How to Tell the Difference Between a Truly Confident Person and an Insecure One Who's Bluffing. Retrieved from https://www.inc.com/minda-zetlin/never-admitting-youre-wrong-confidence-insecurity-mistakes.html

Zetlin, M. (2020b, February 6). Want to Be More Confident? 9 Ways to Overcome Your Own Fears. Retrieved from https://www.inc.com/minda-zetlin/9-ways-being-afraid-can-make-you-a-stronger-leader.html

Printed in Great Britain
by Amazon